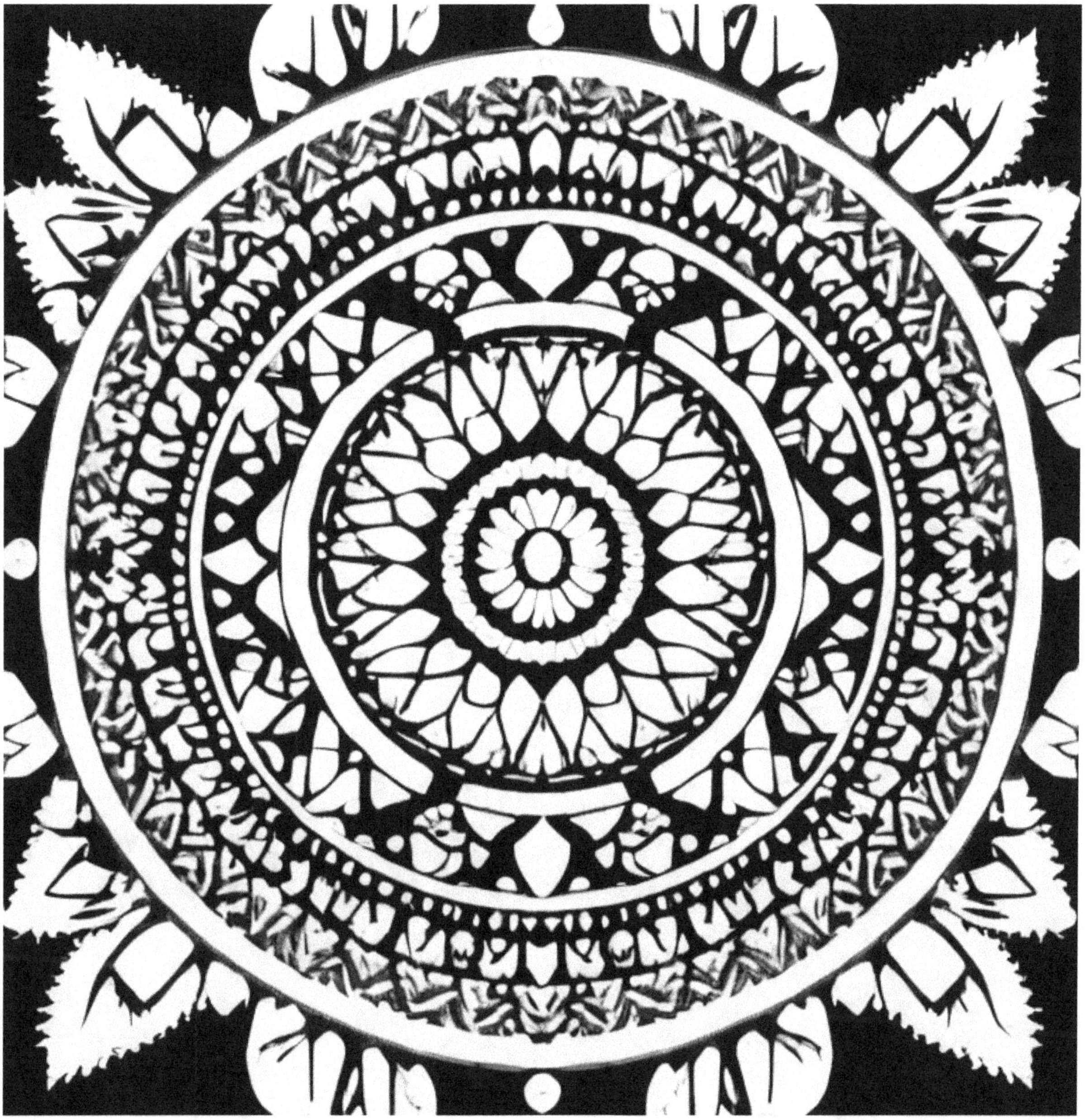

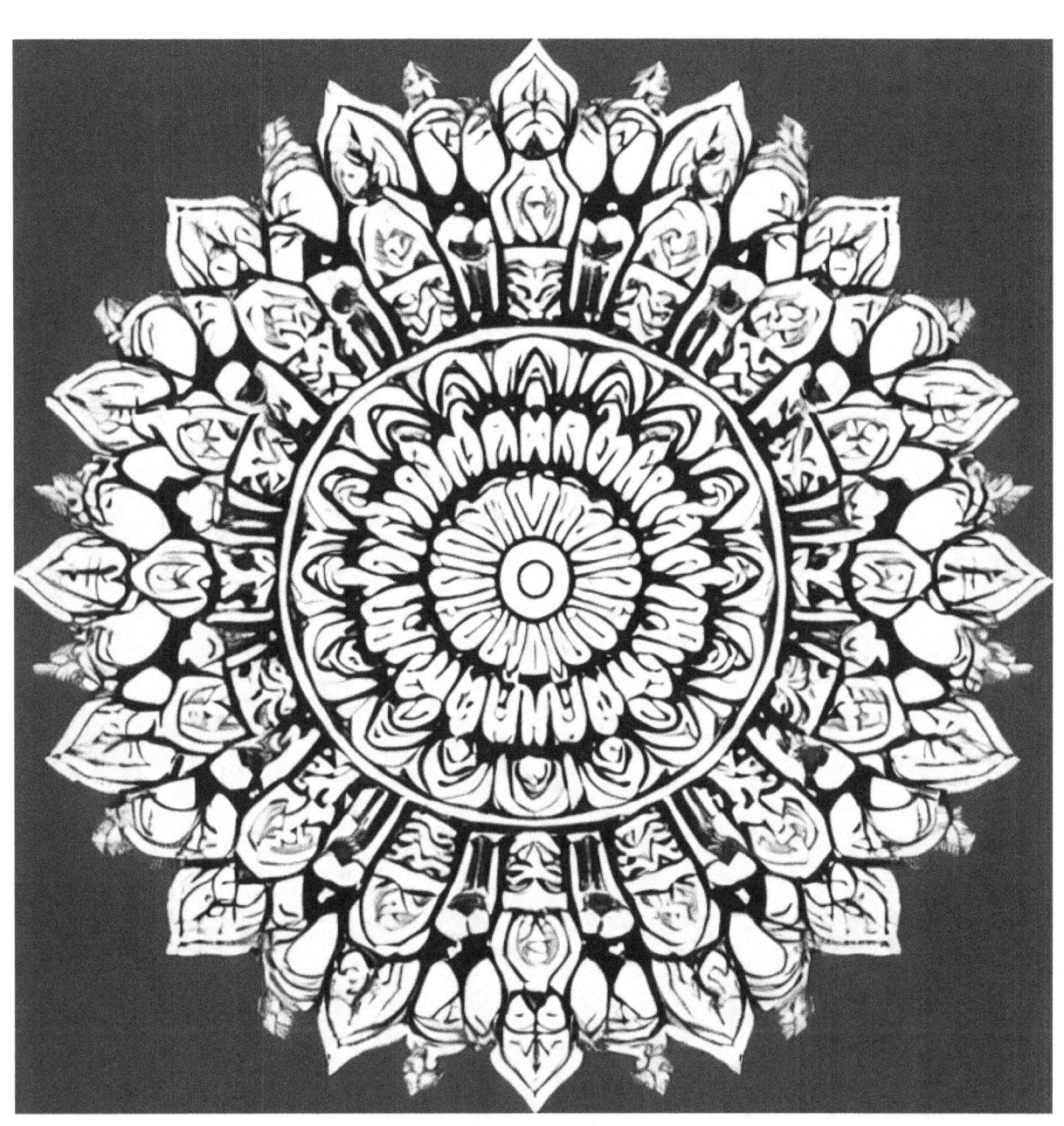

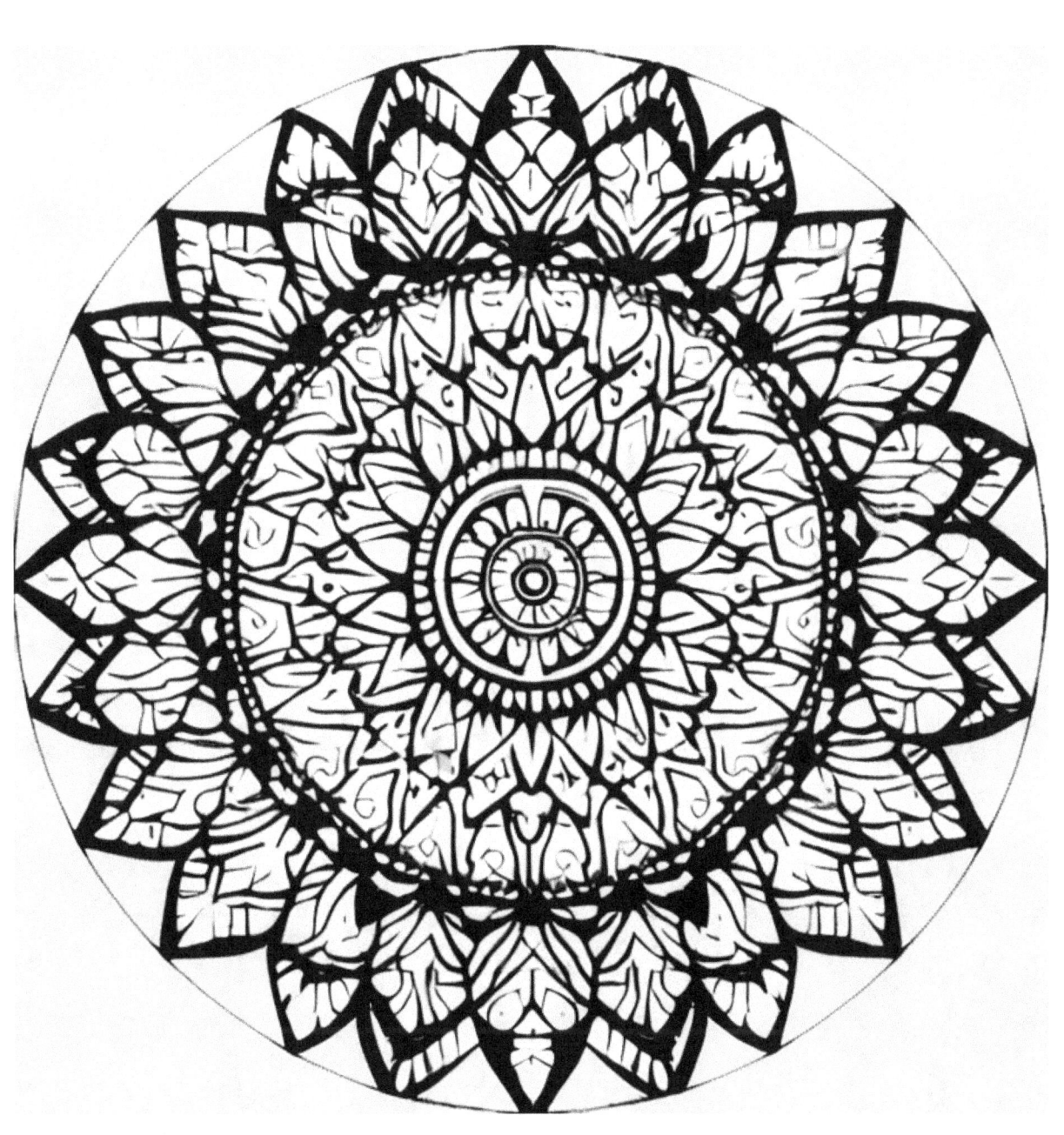

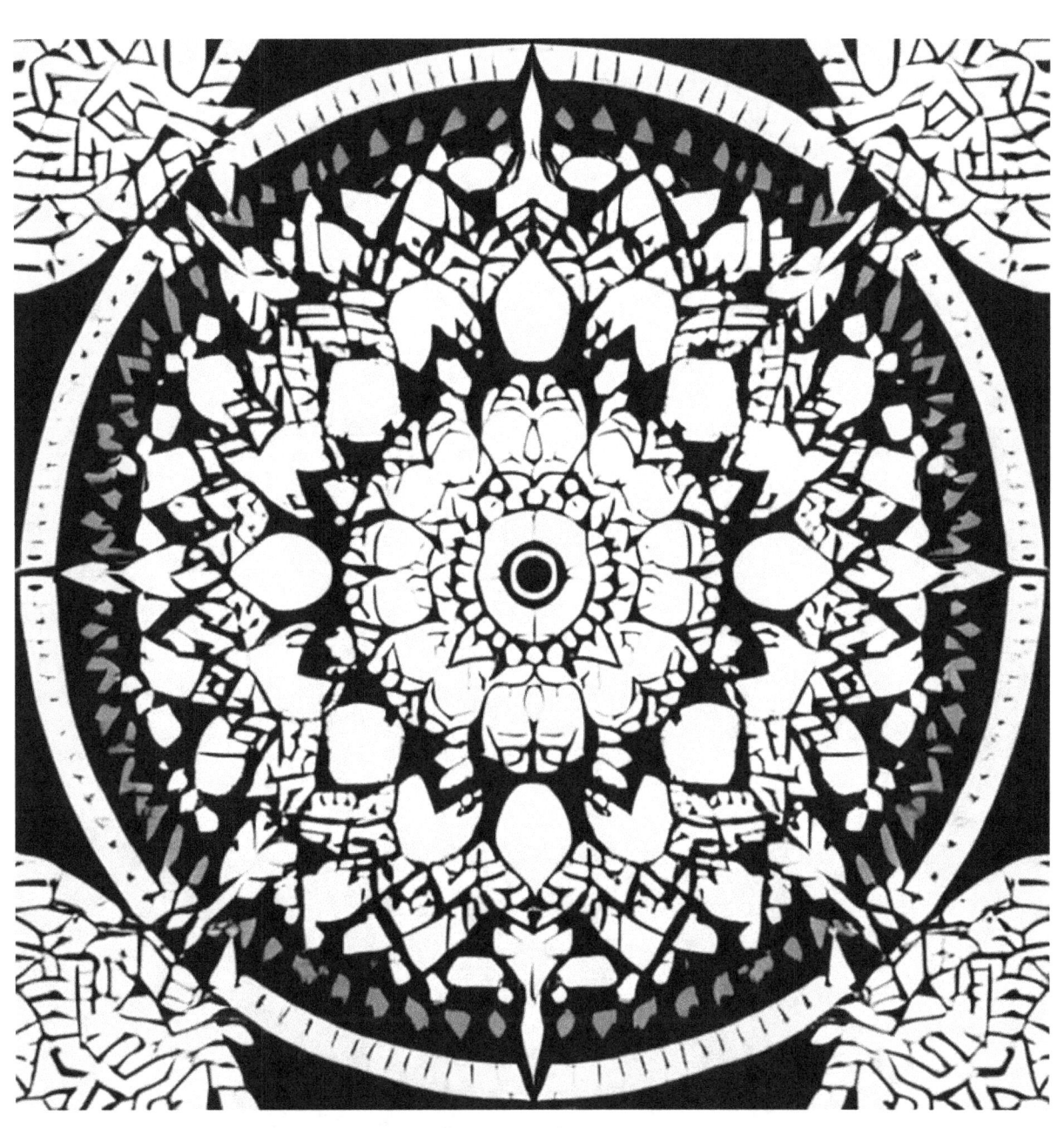

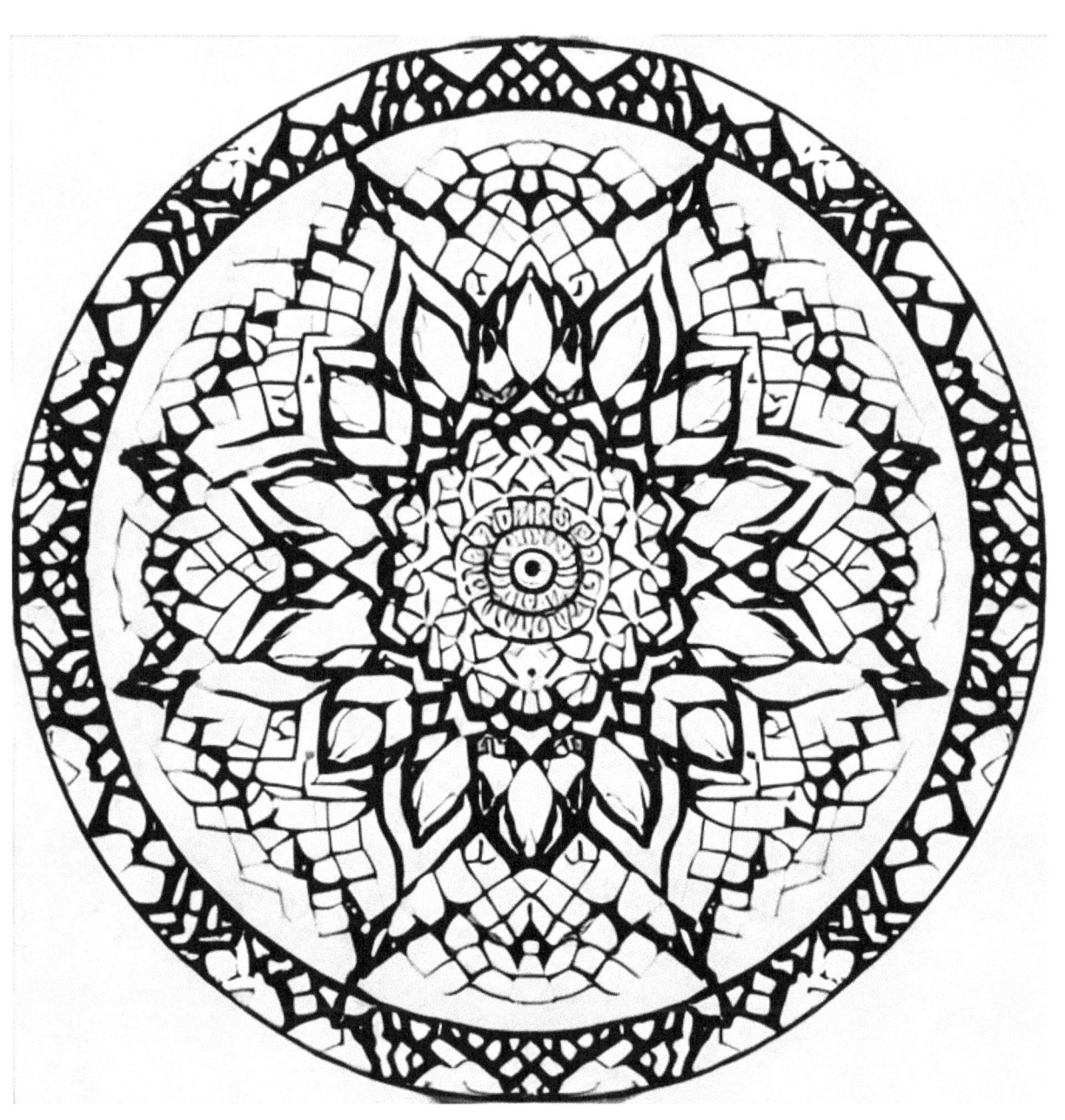

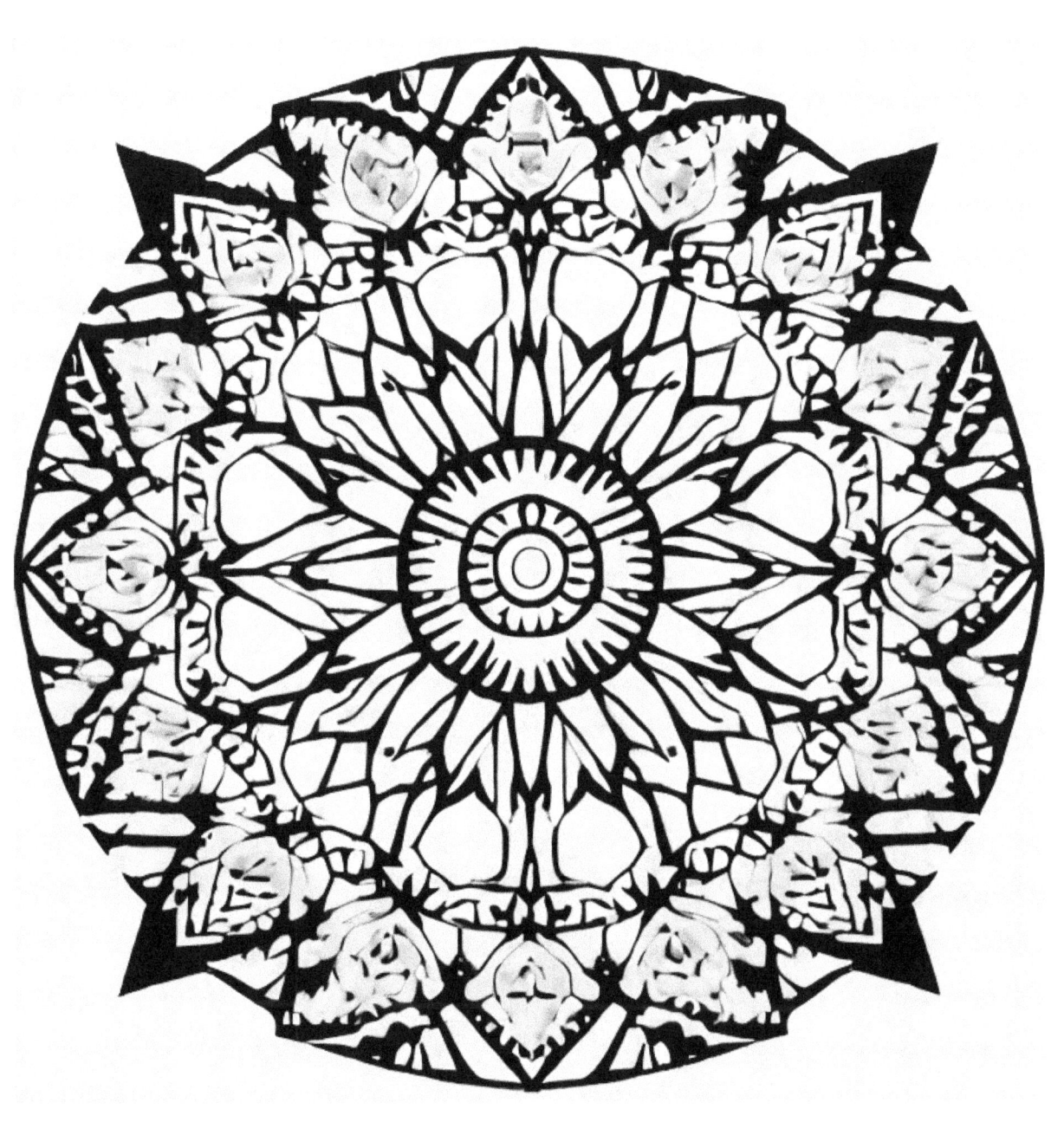

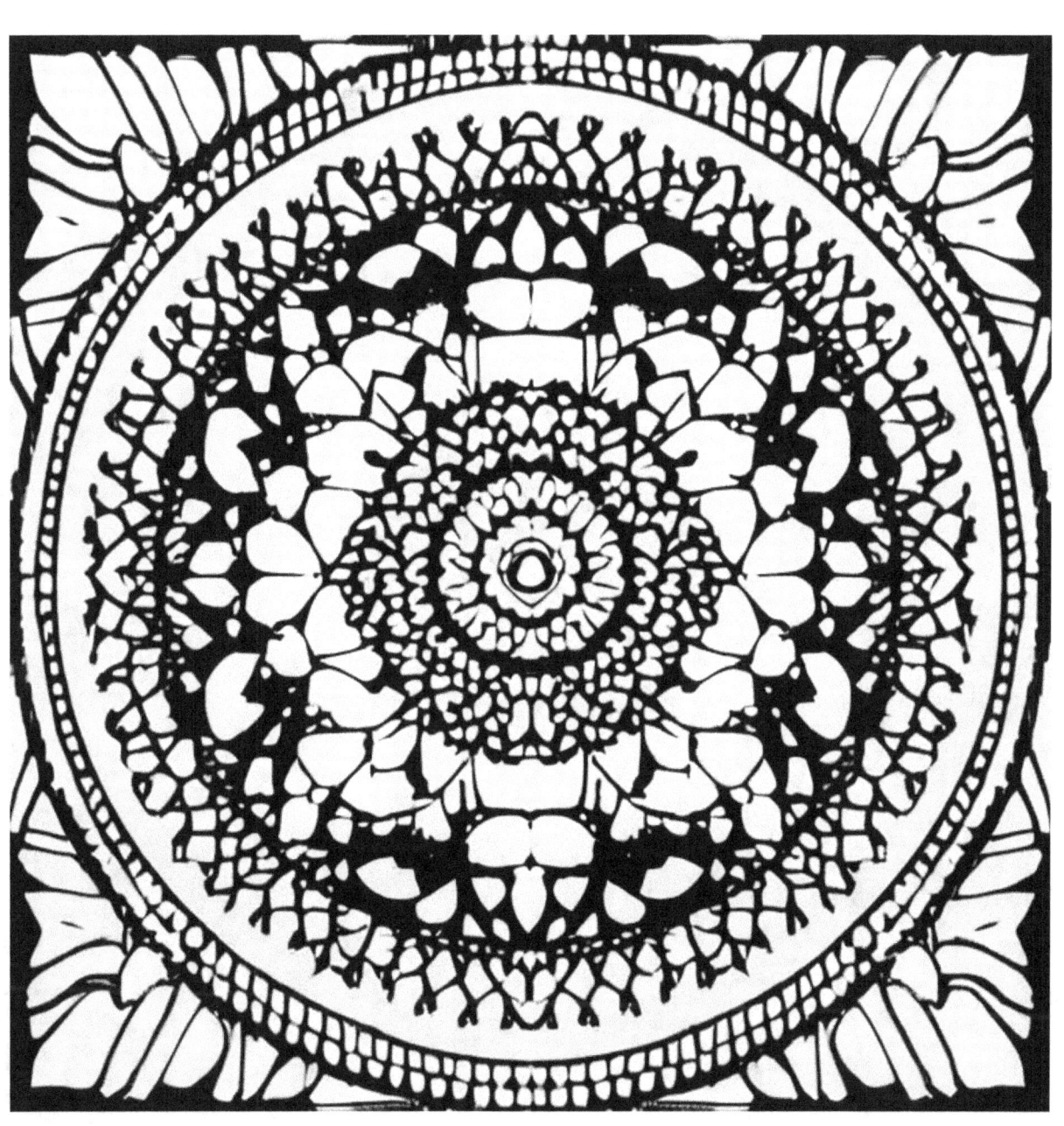

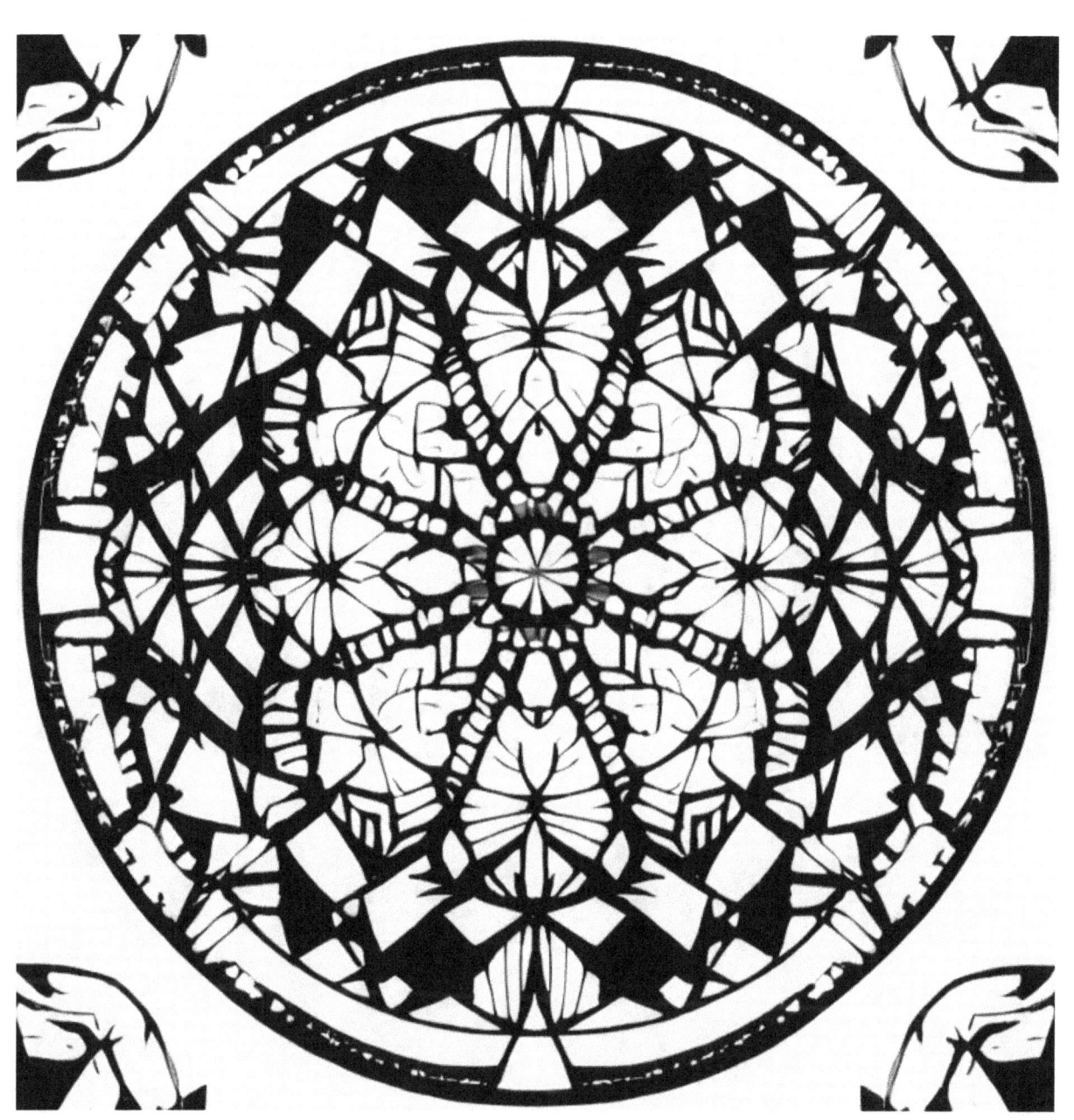

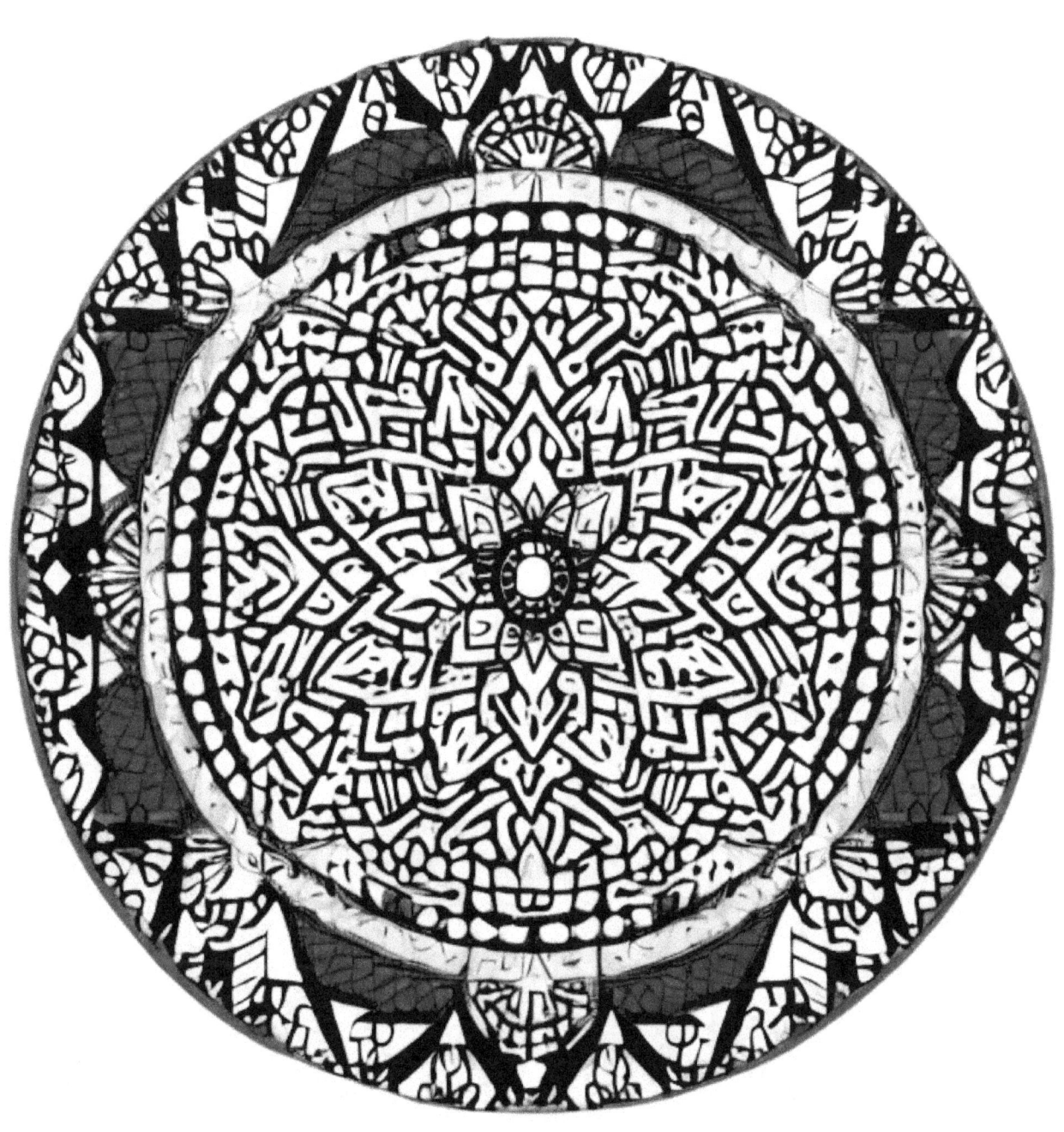

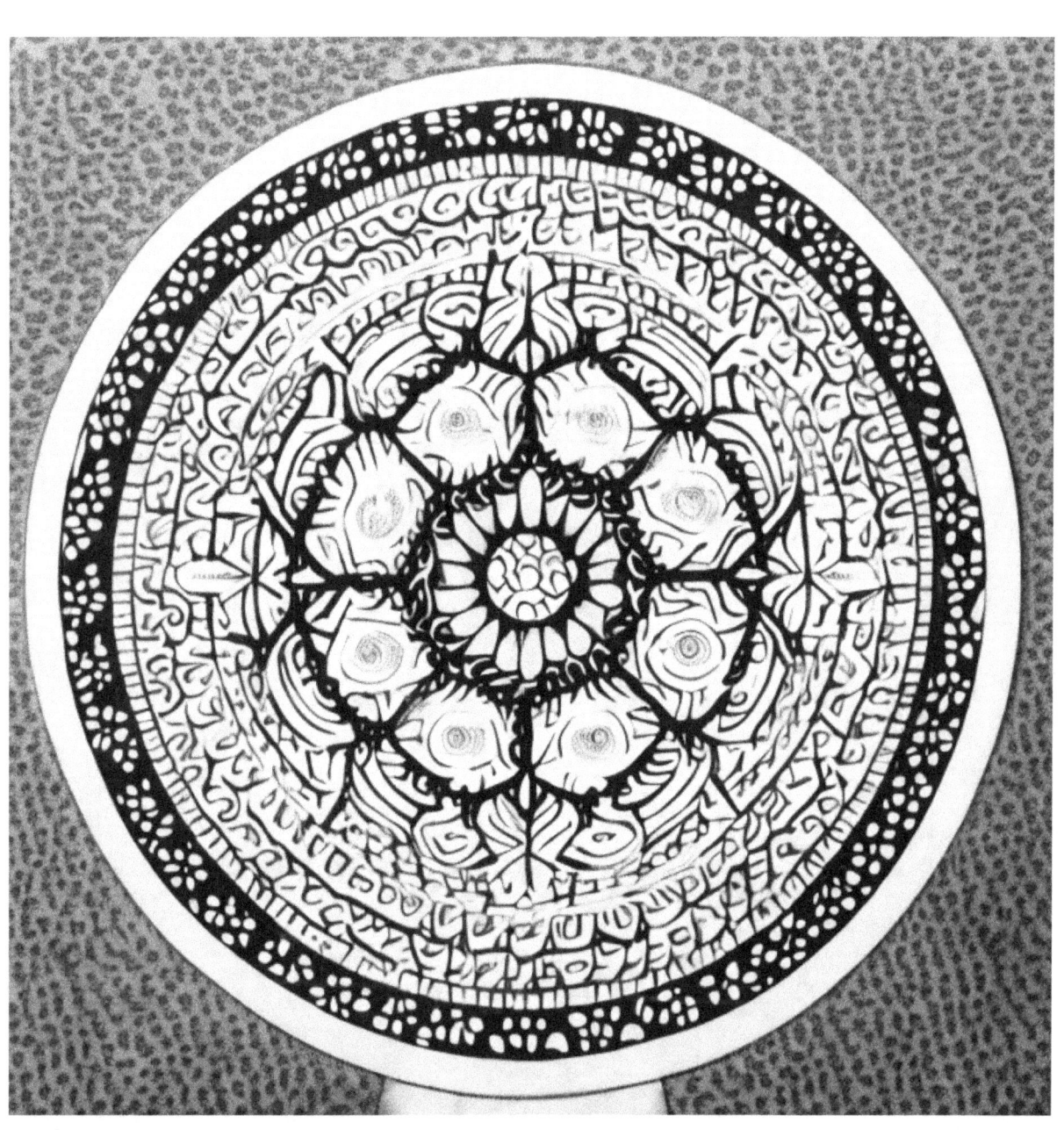

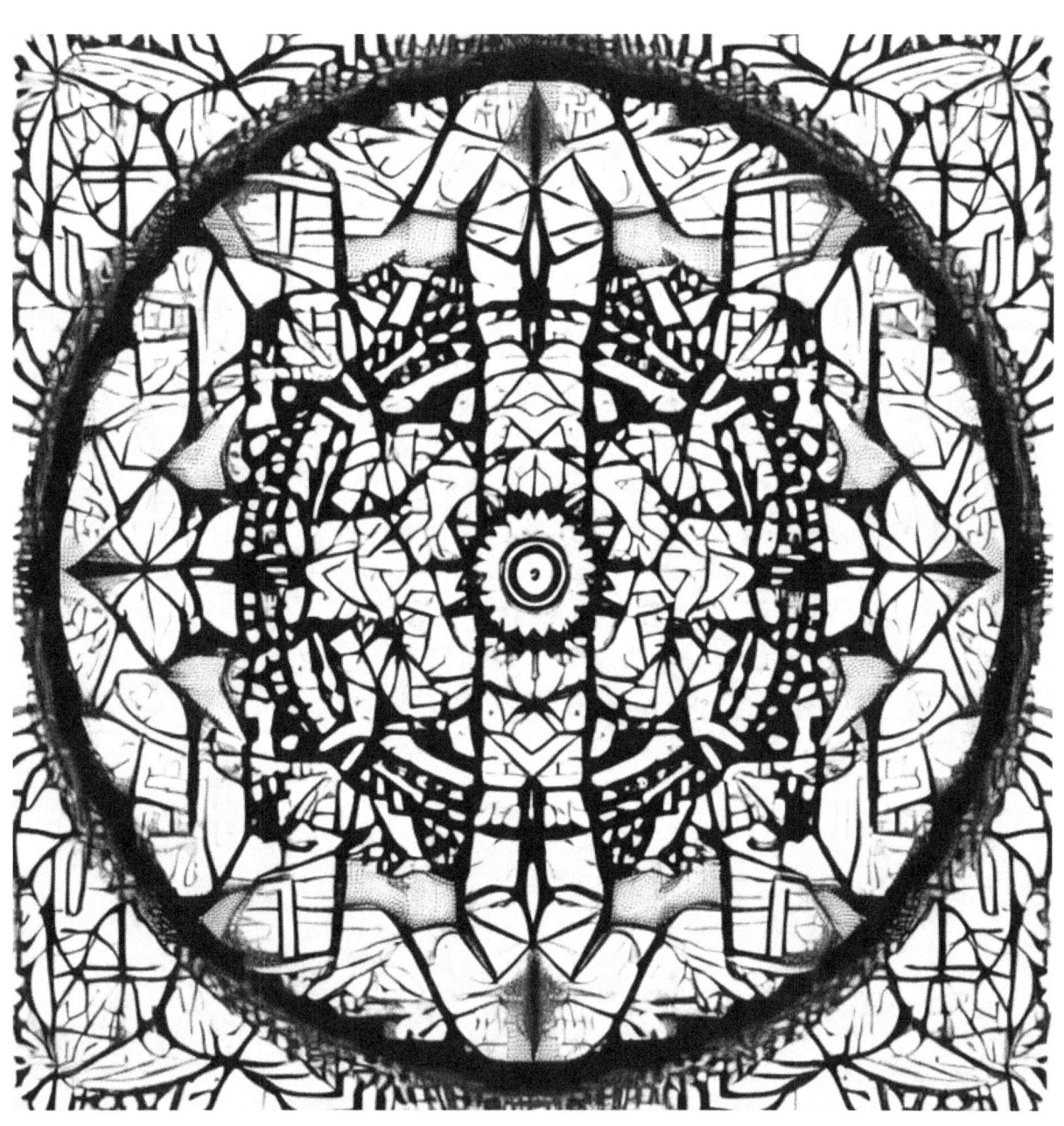

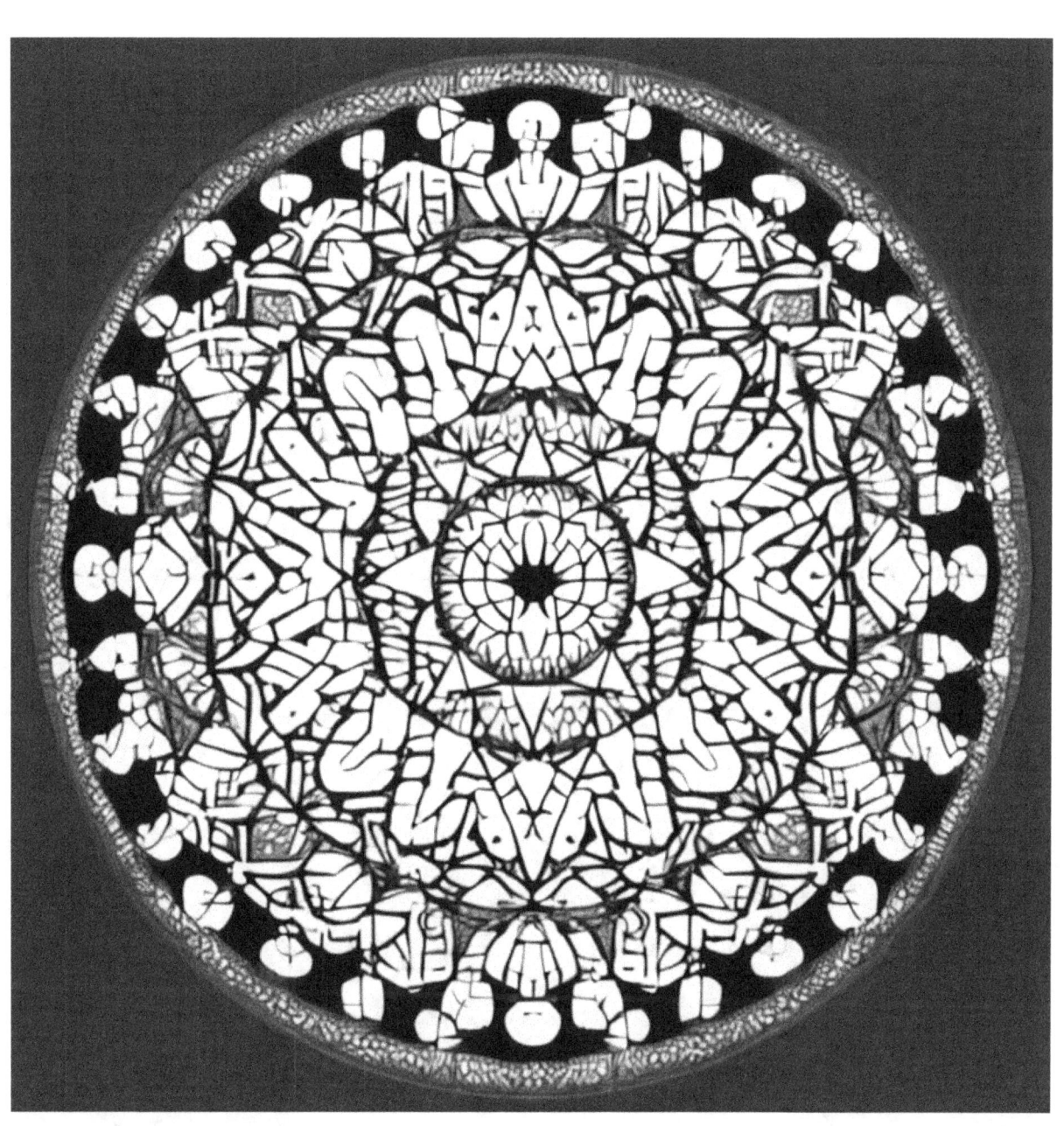

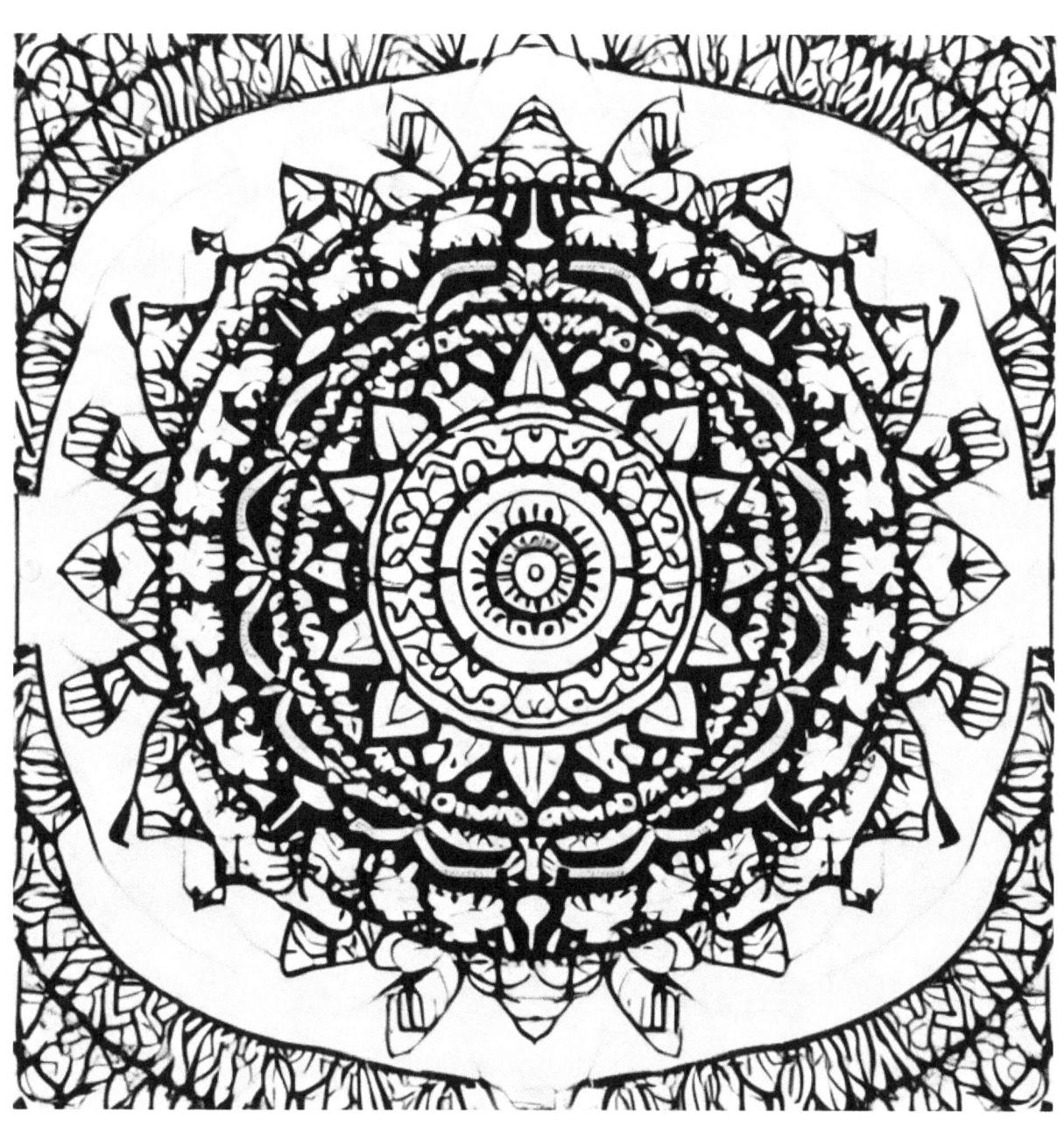

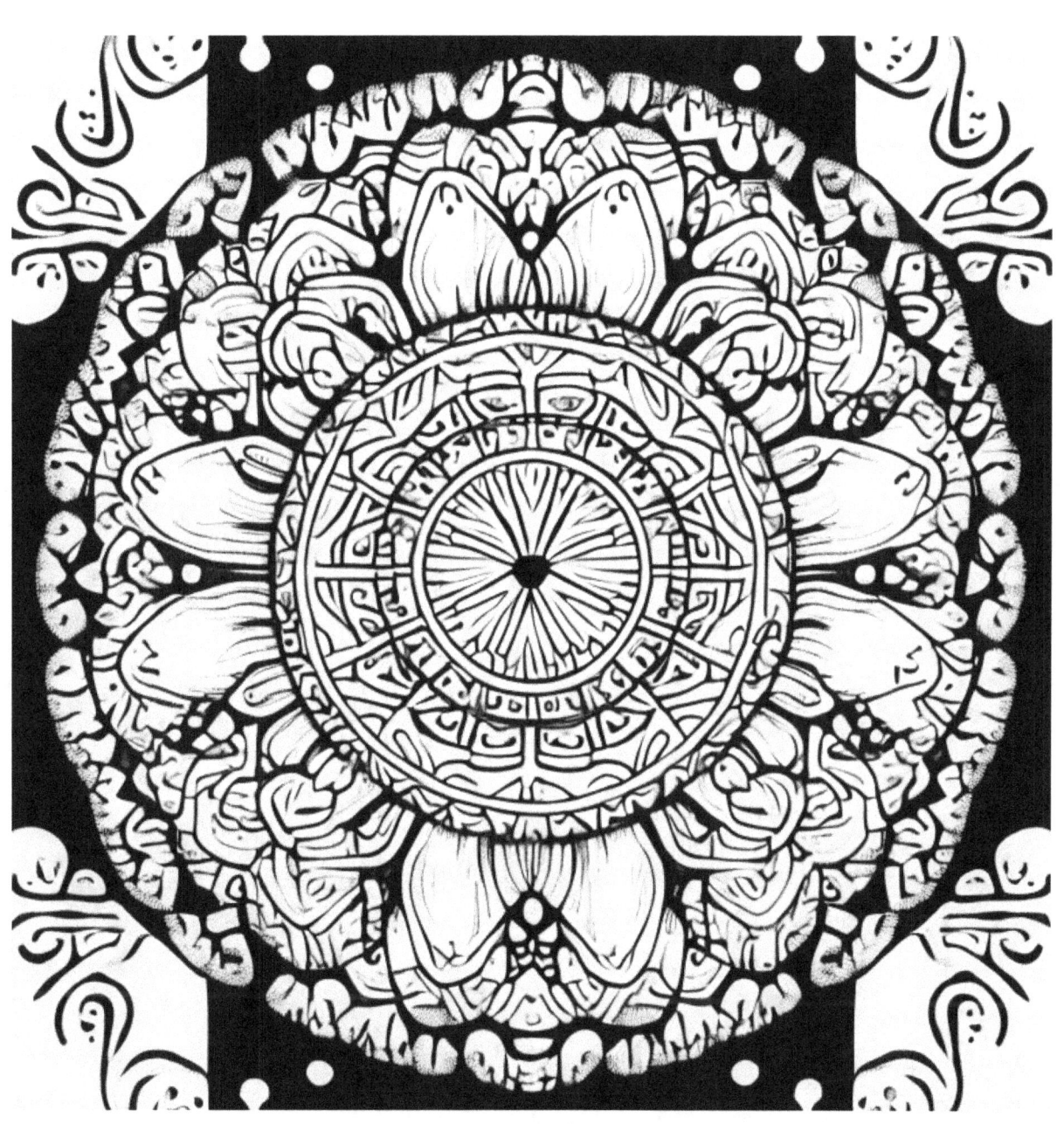

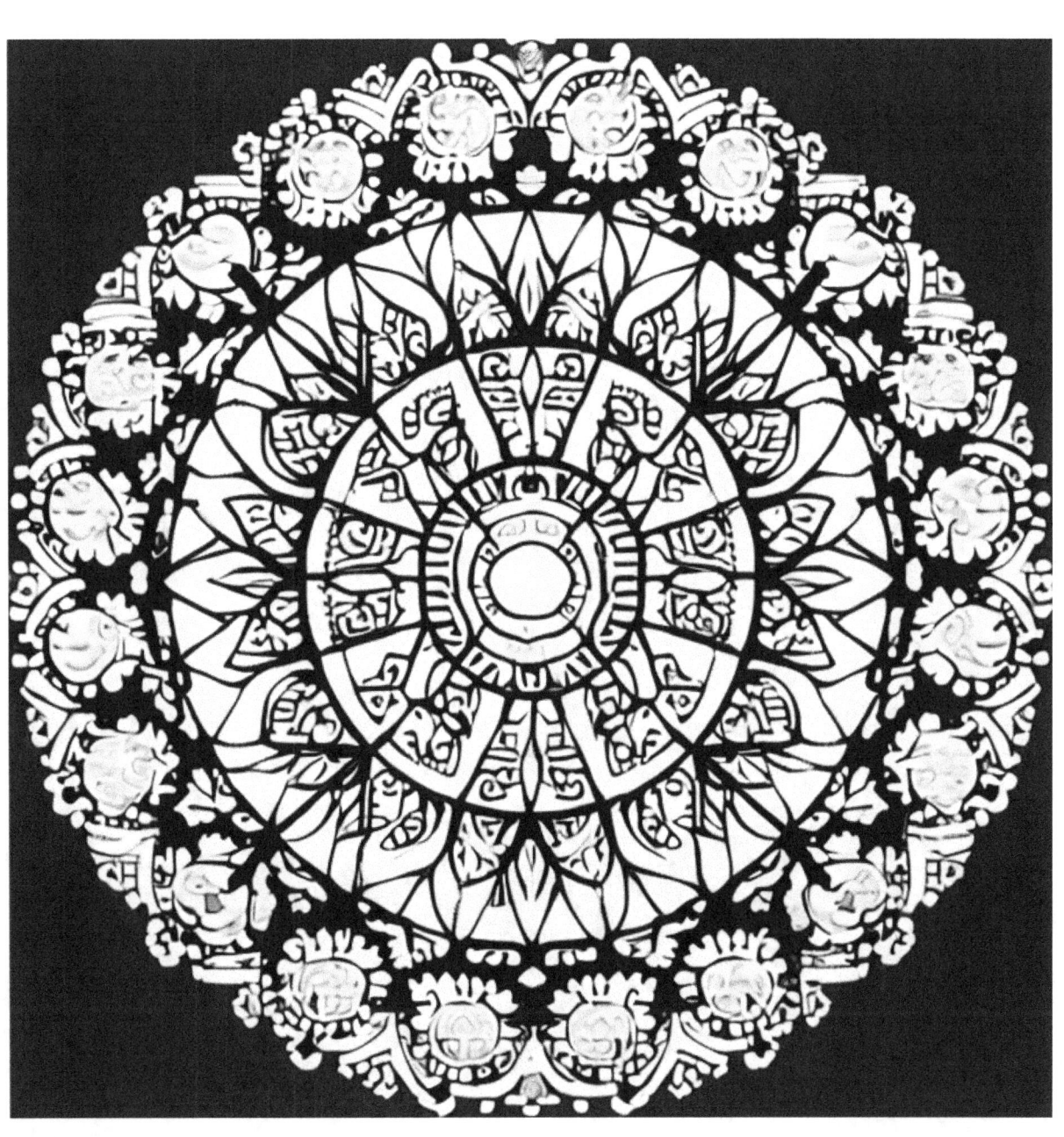

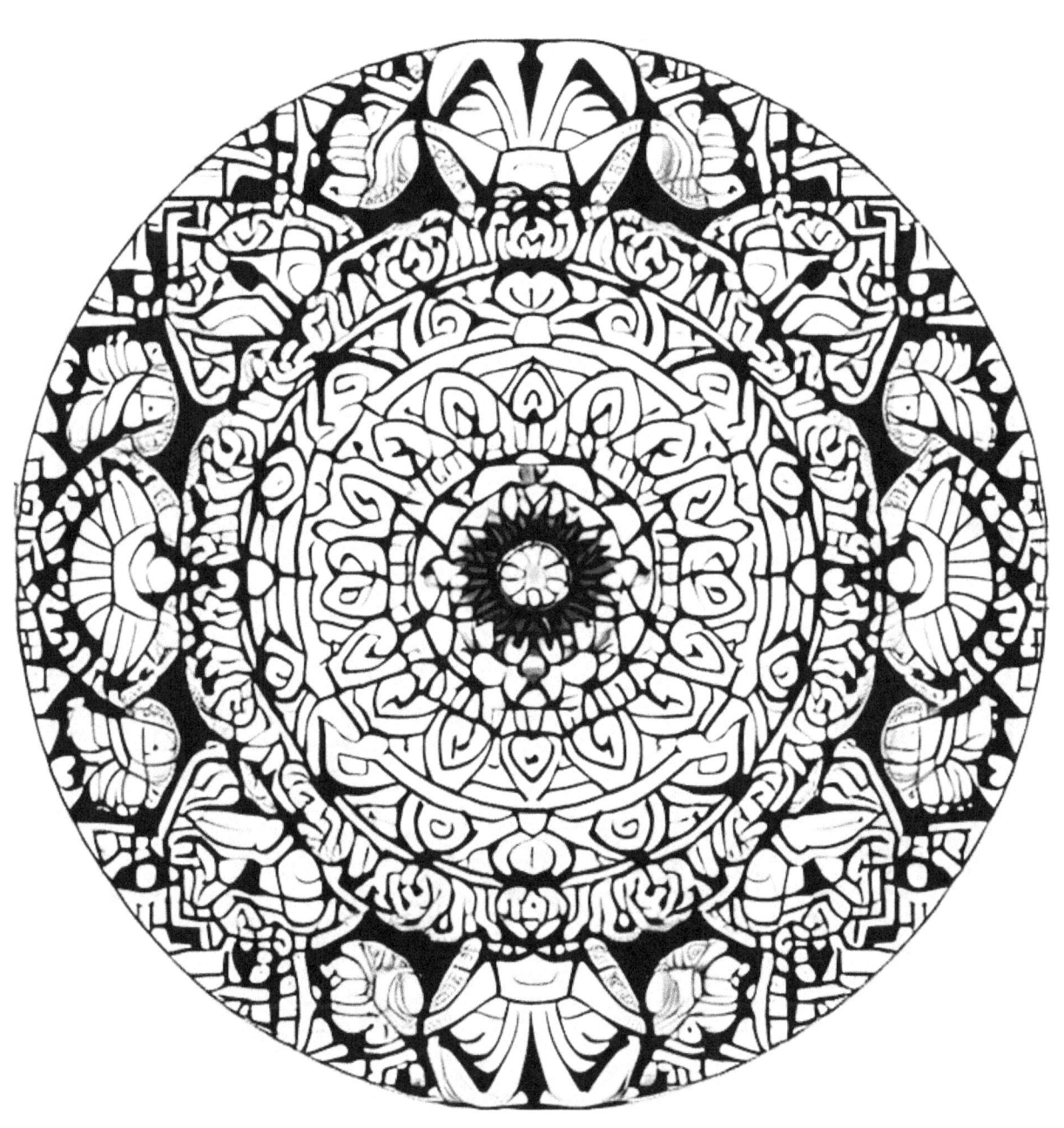

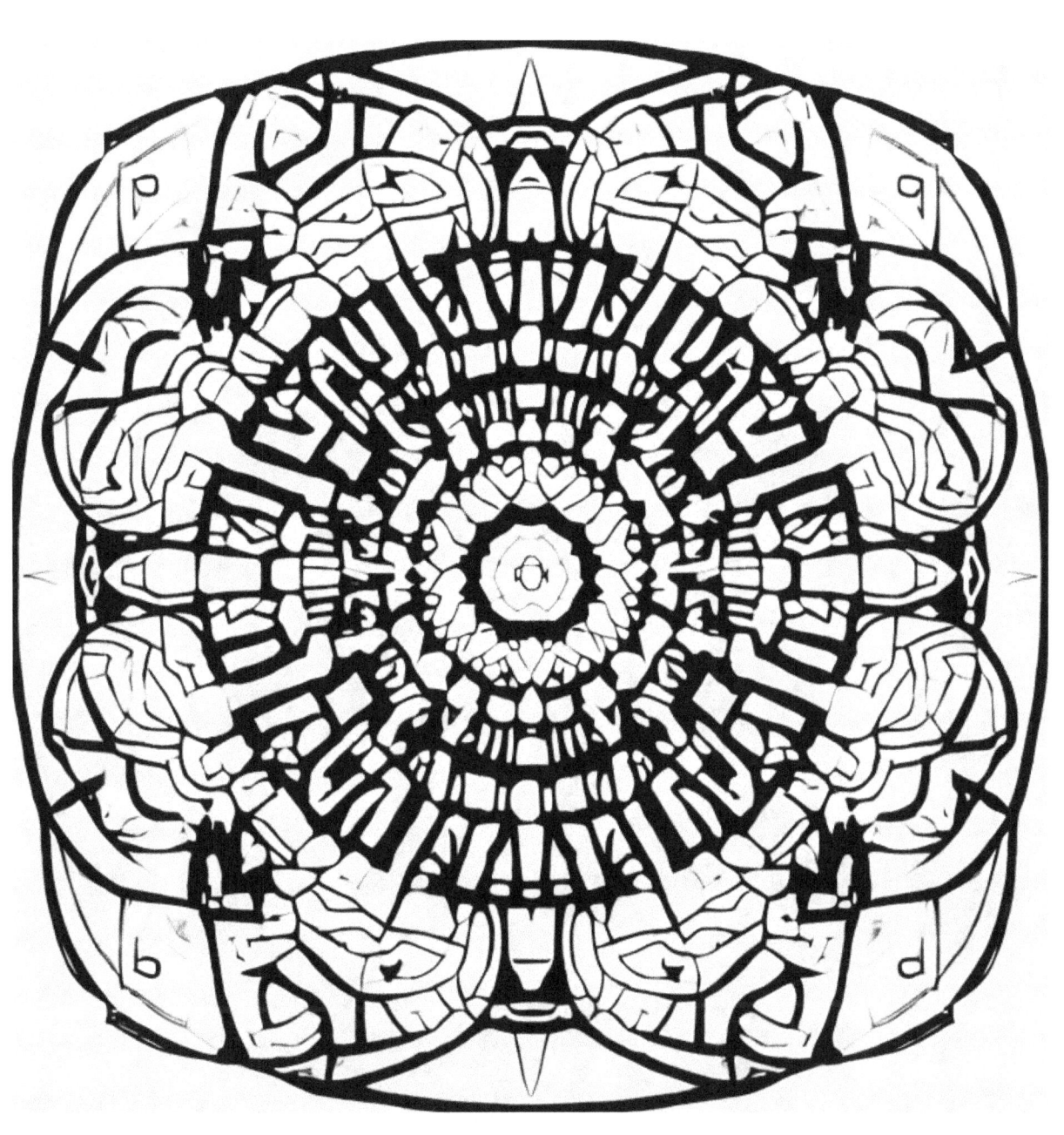

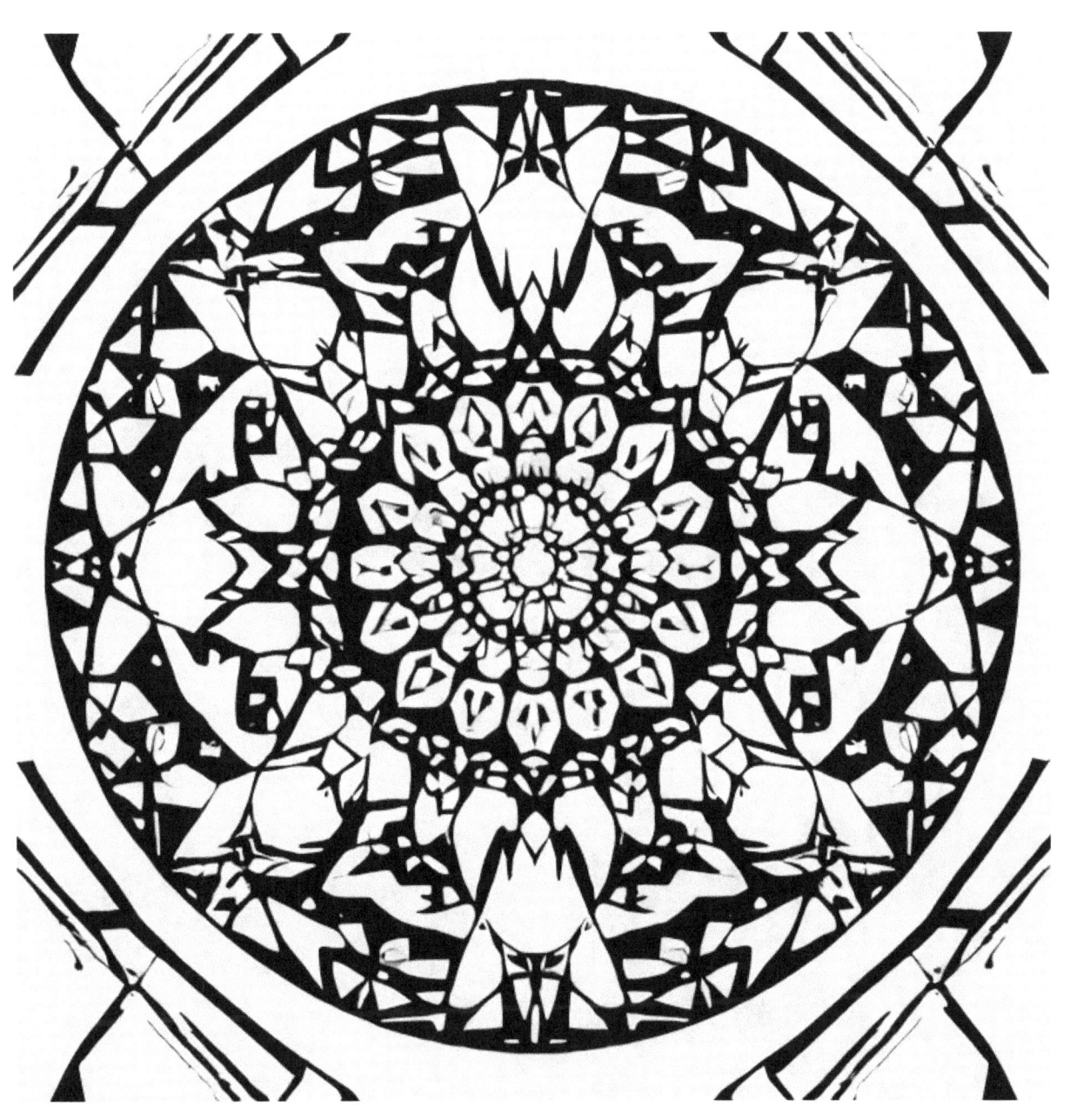

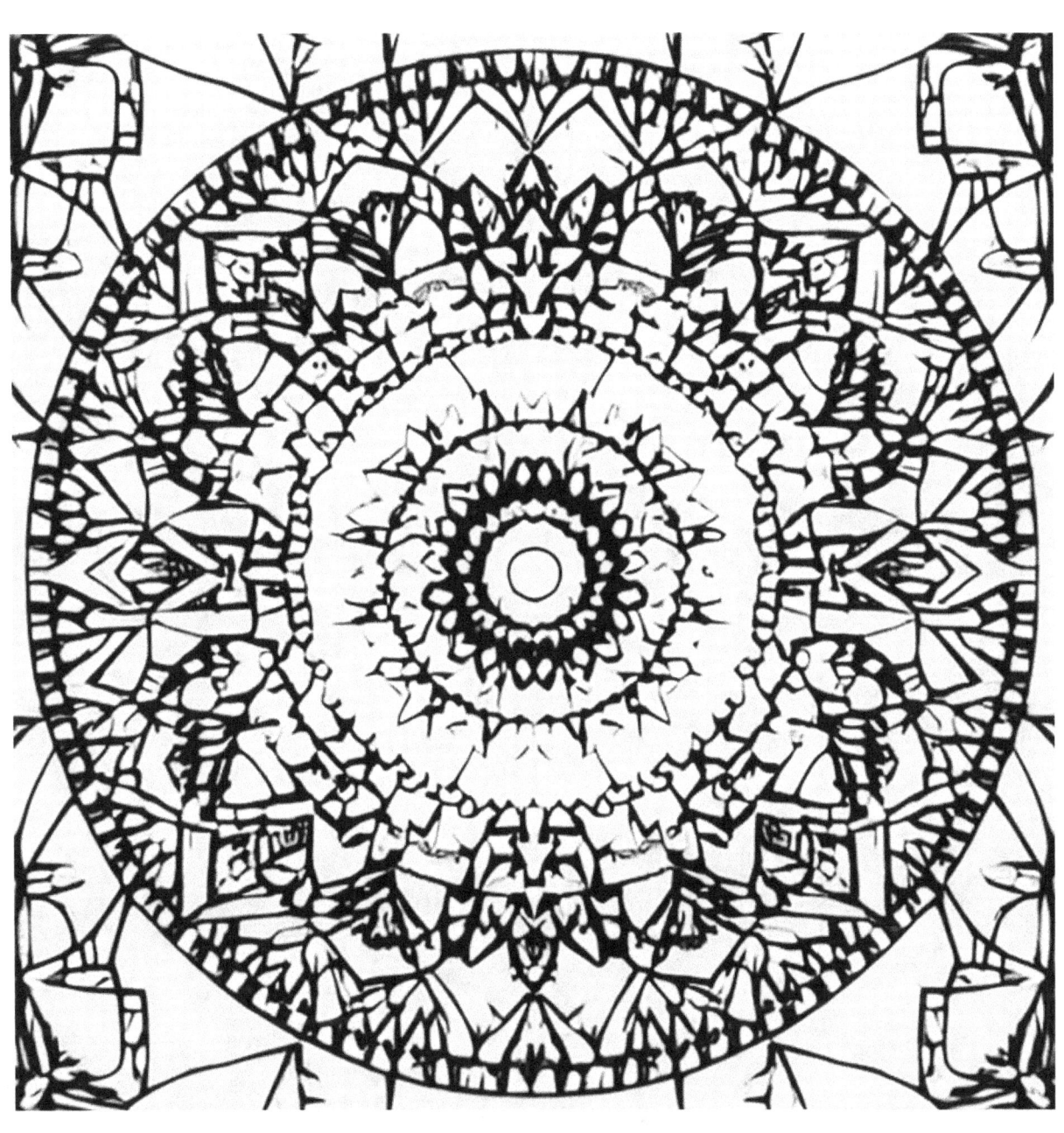

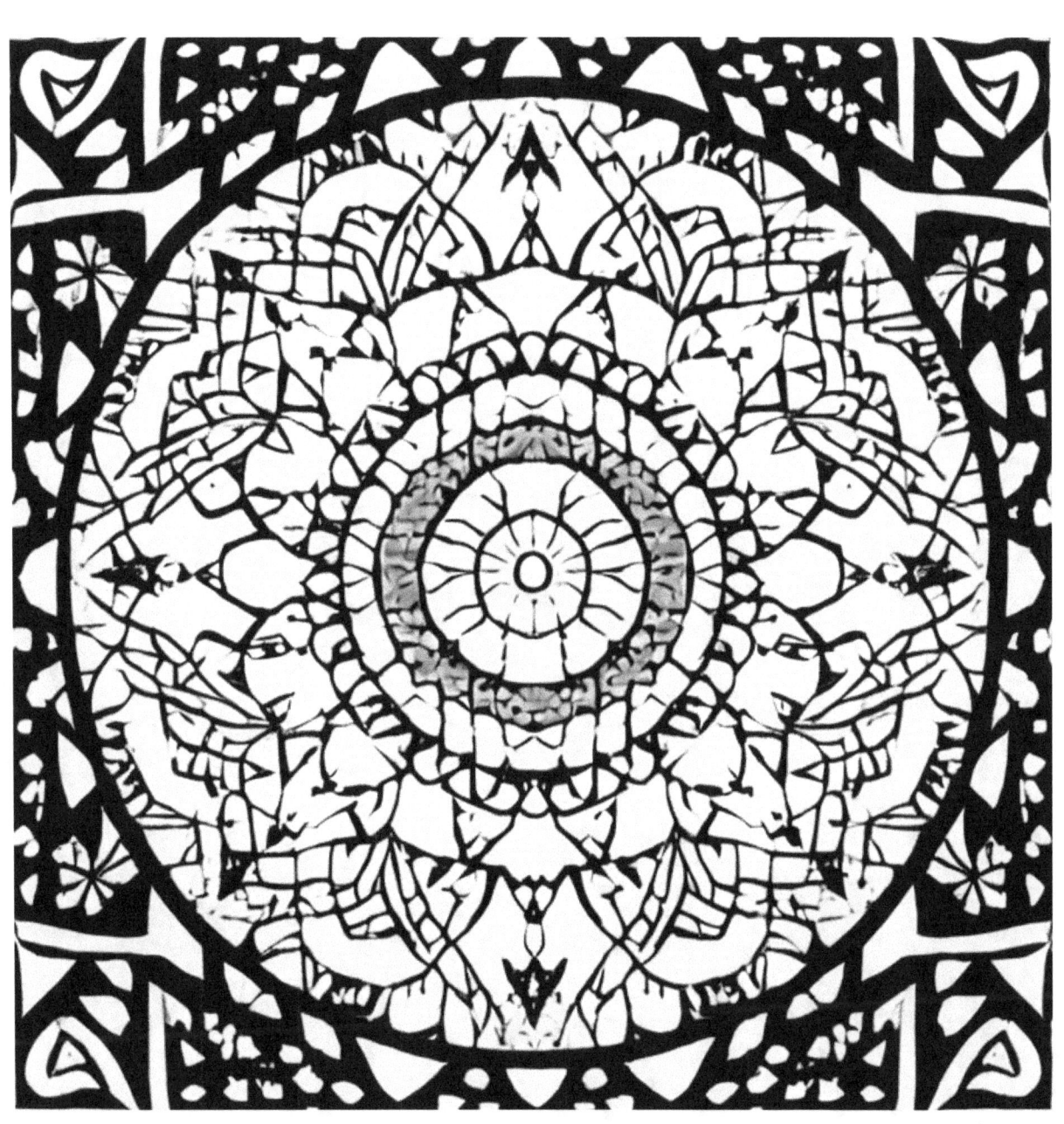

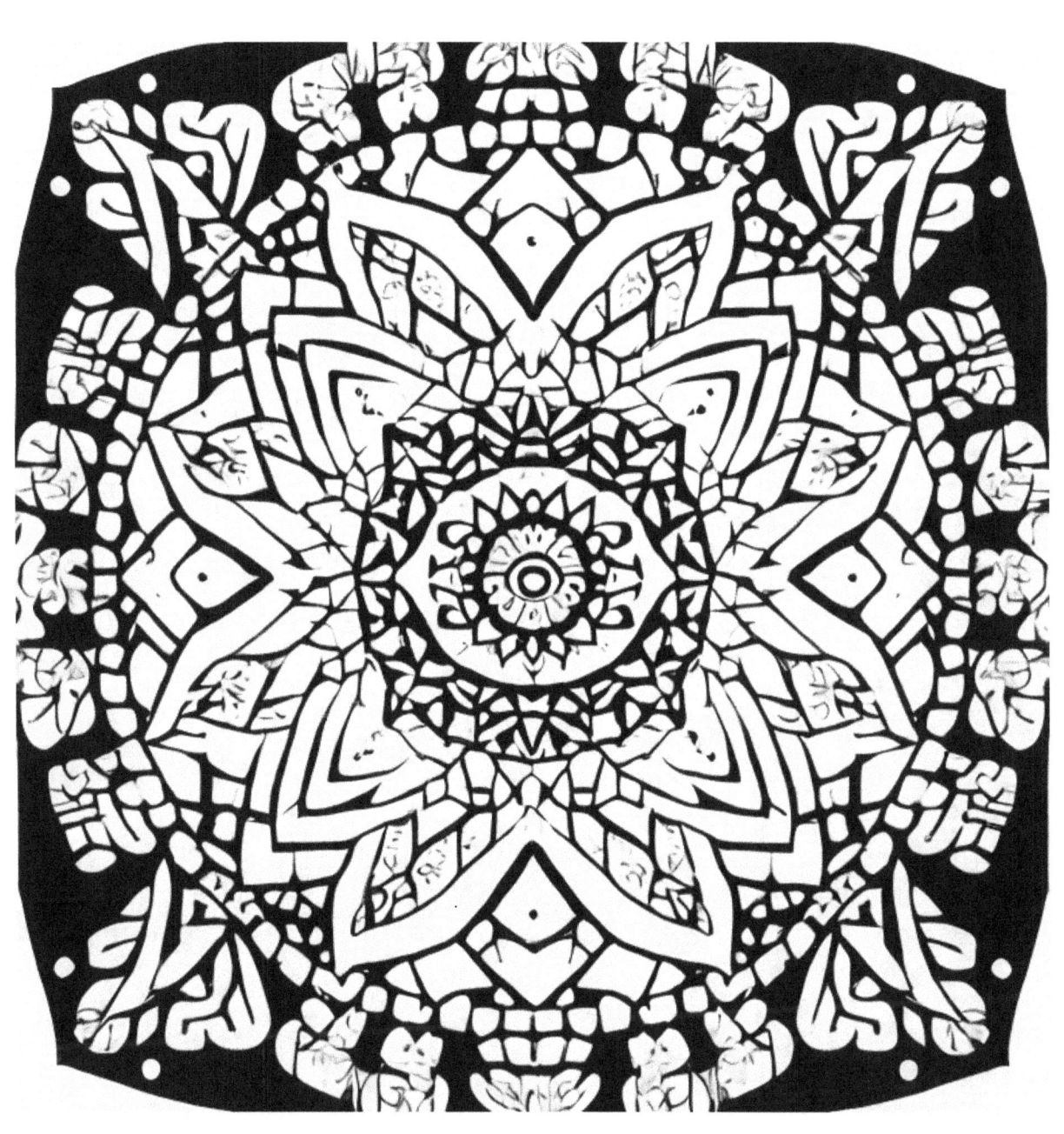

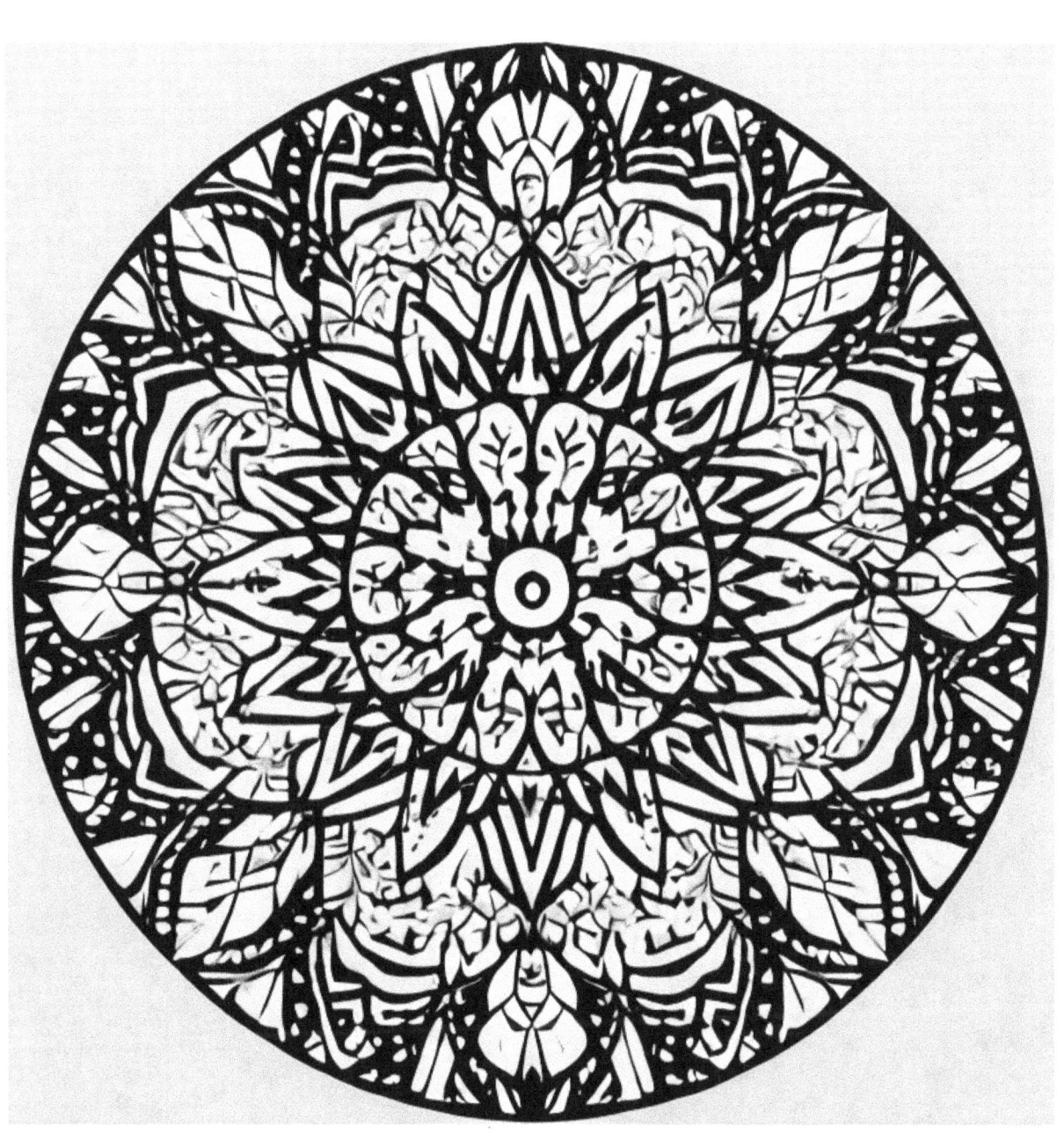

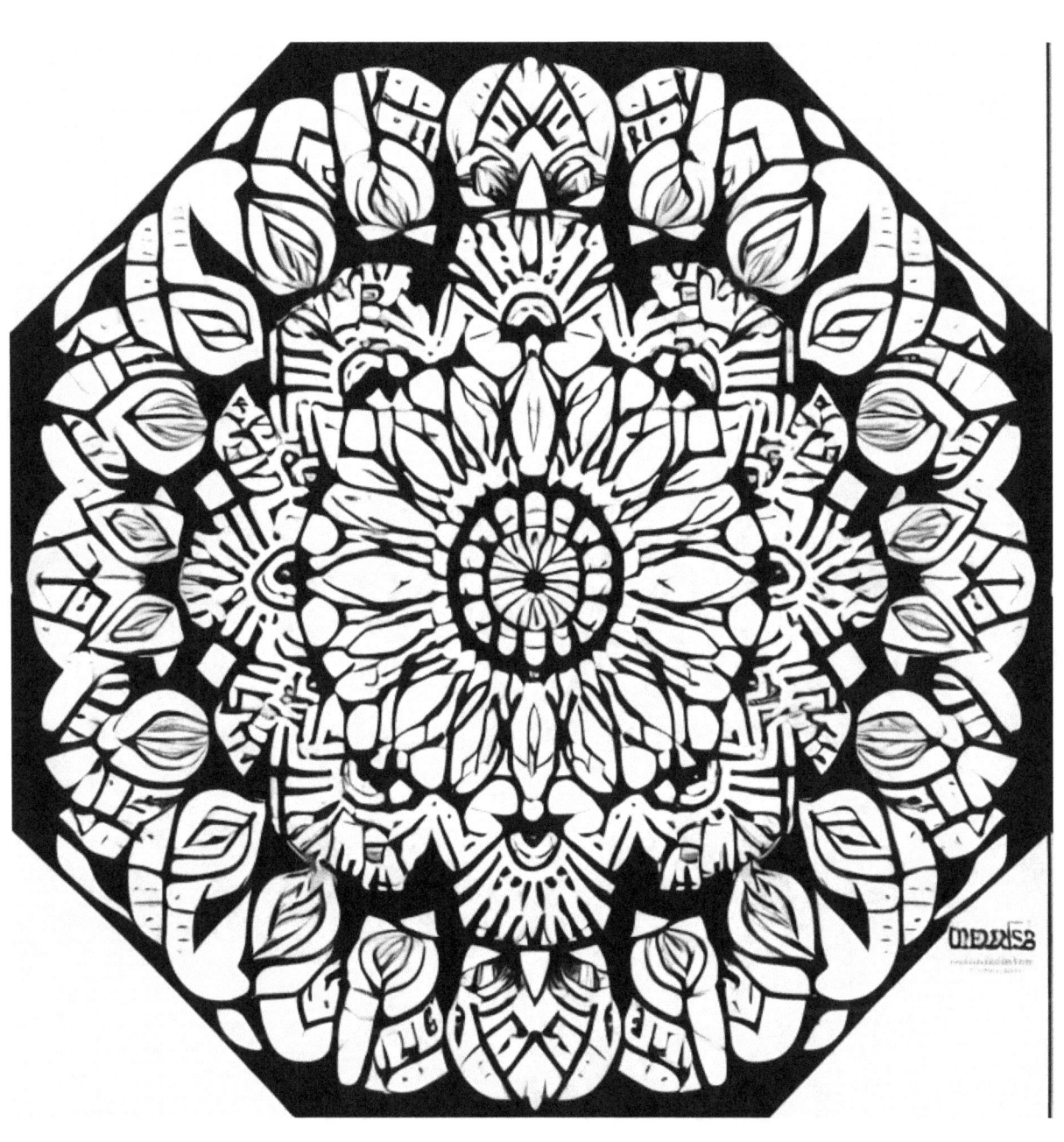

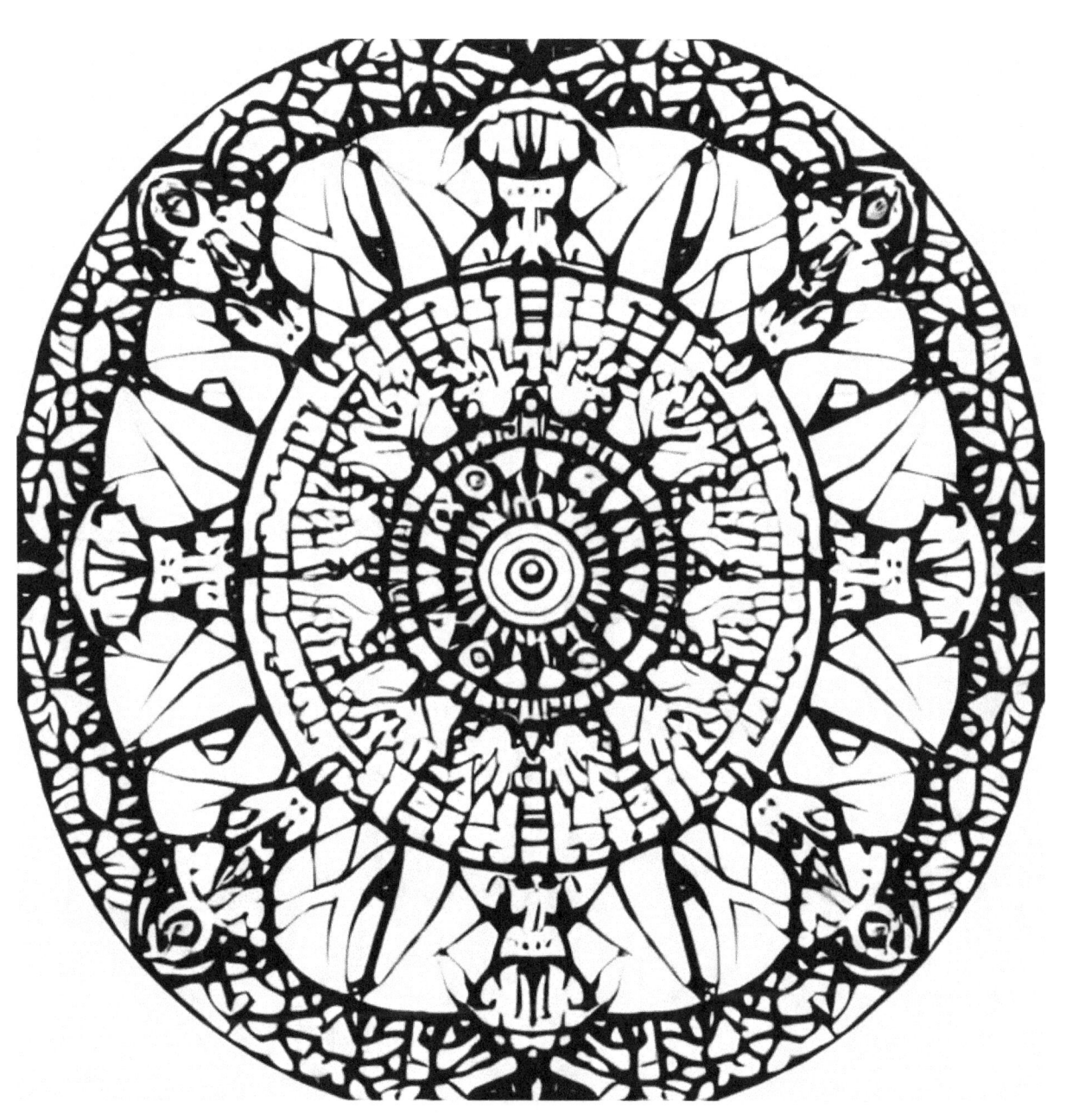

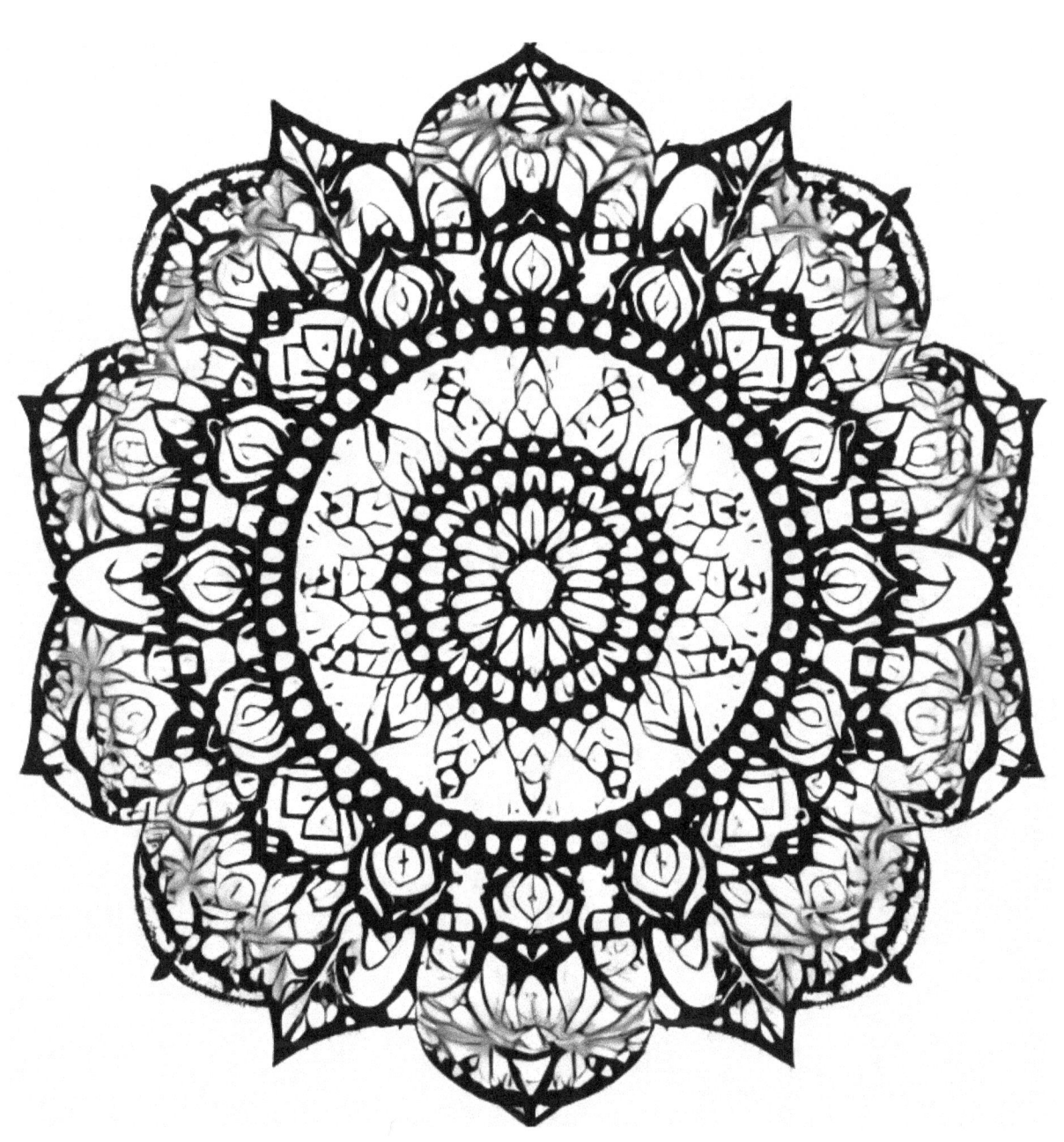

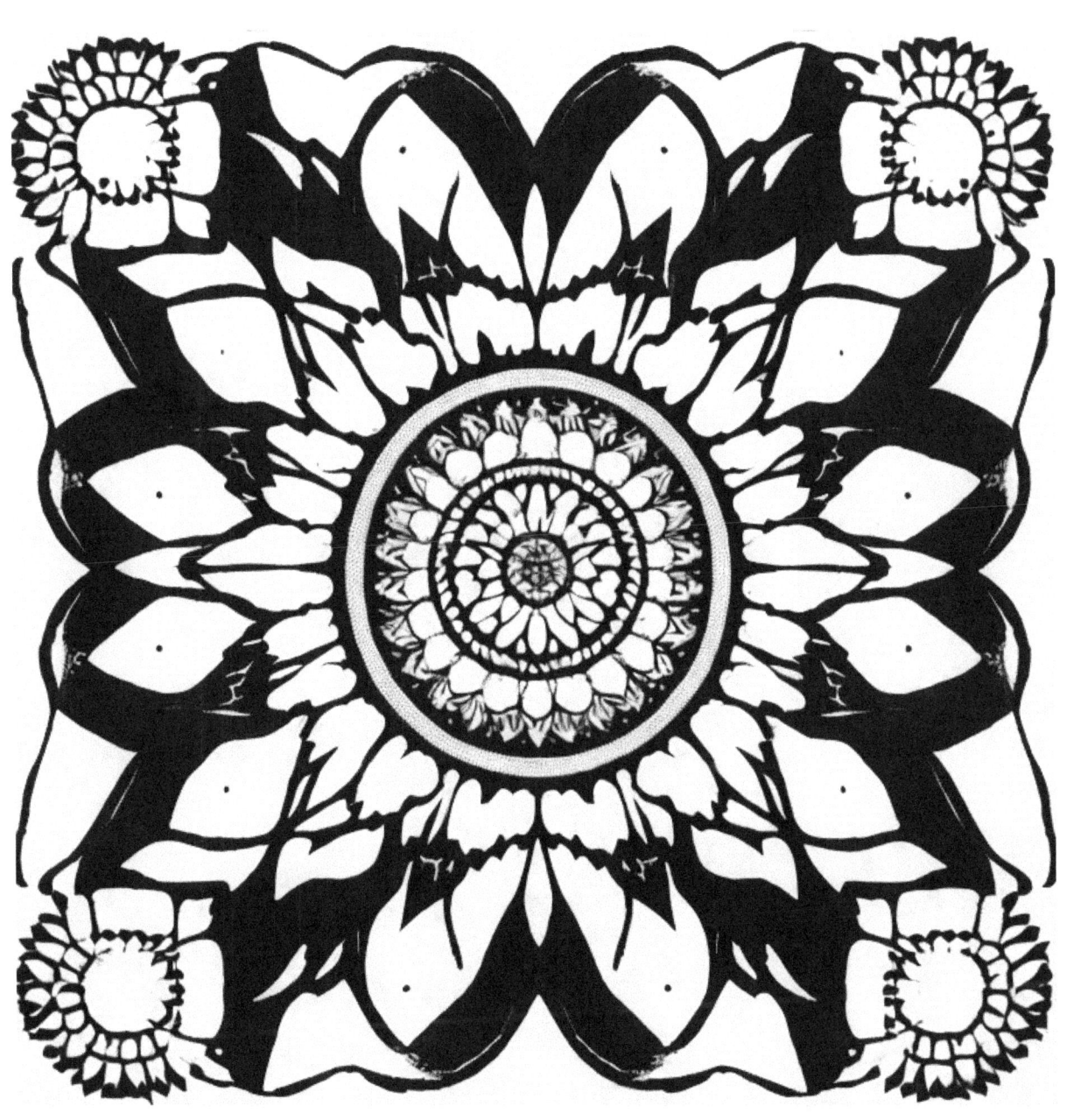

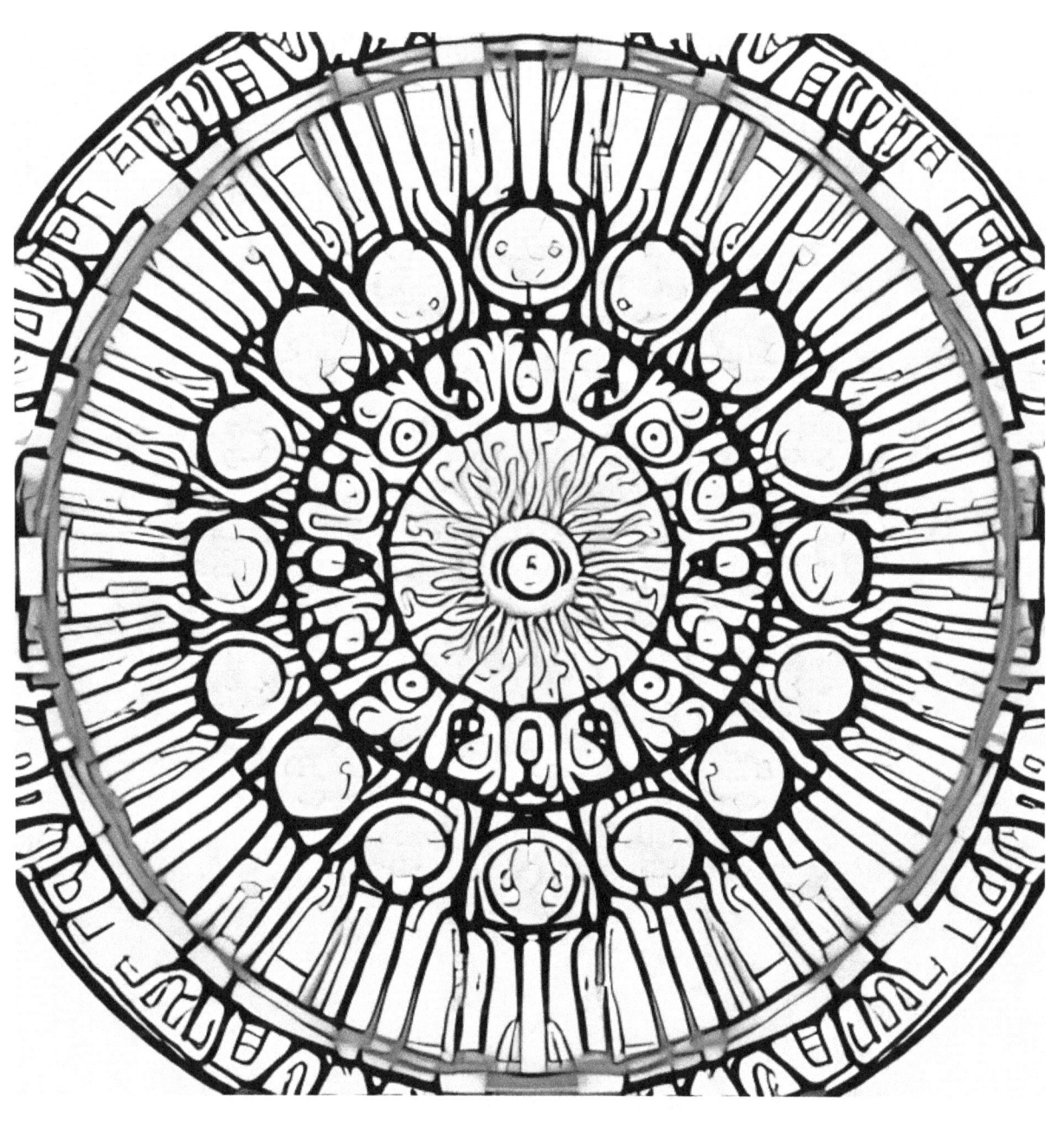

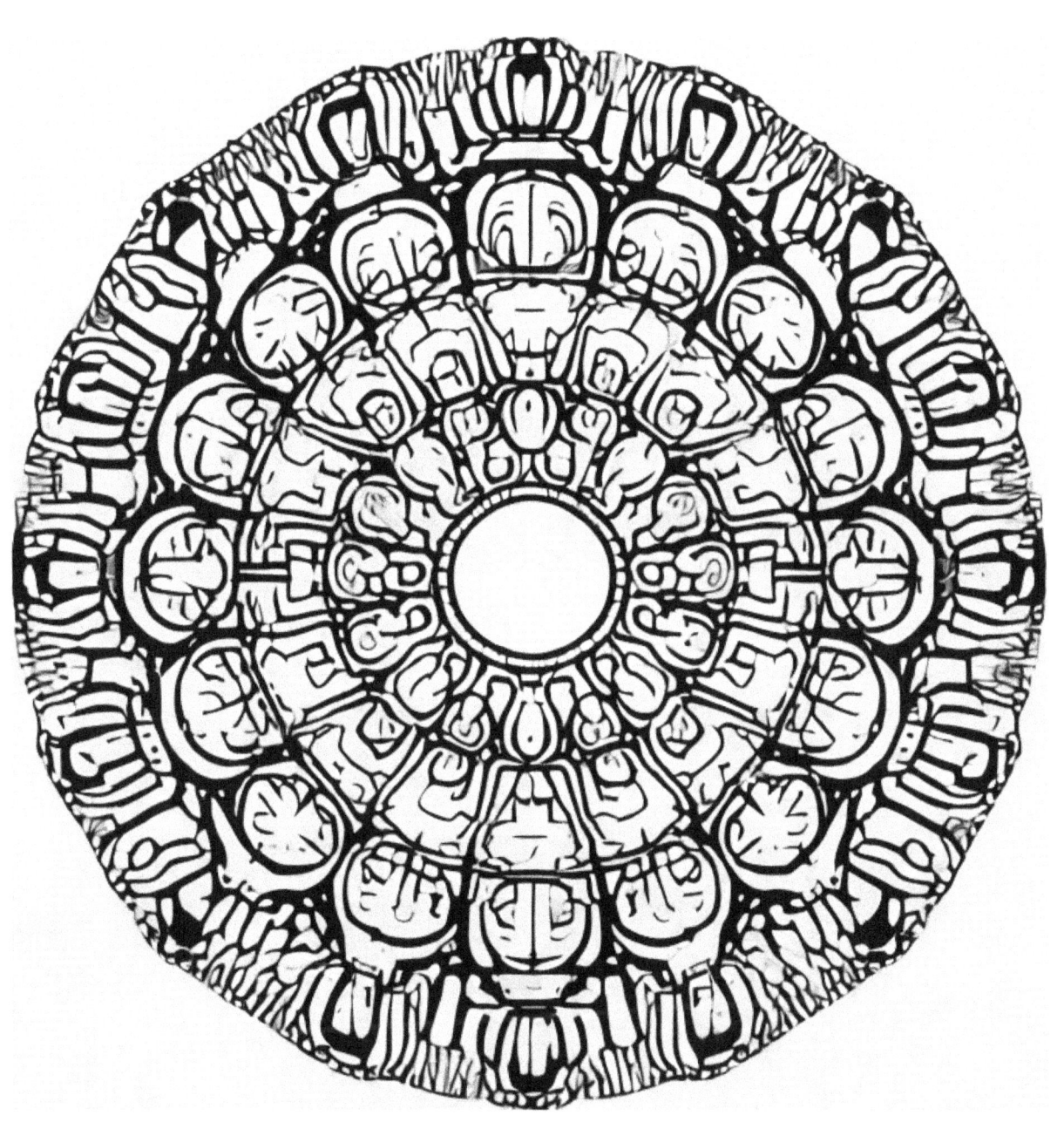

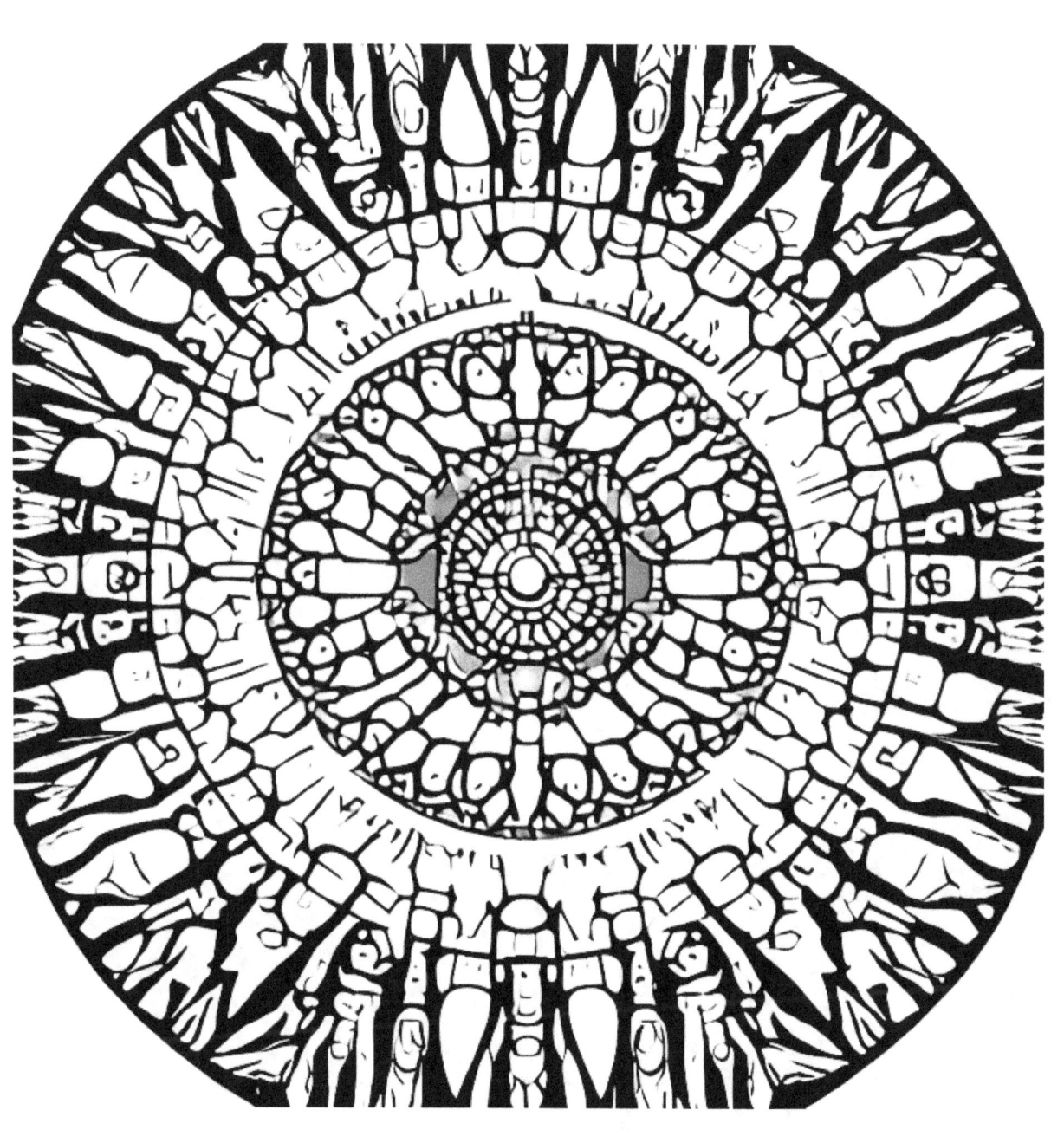

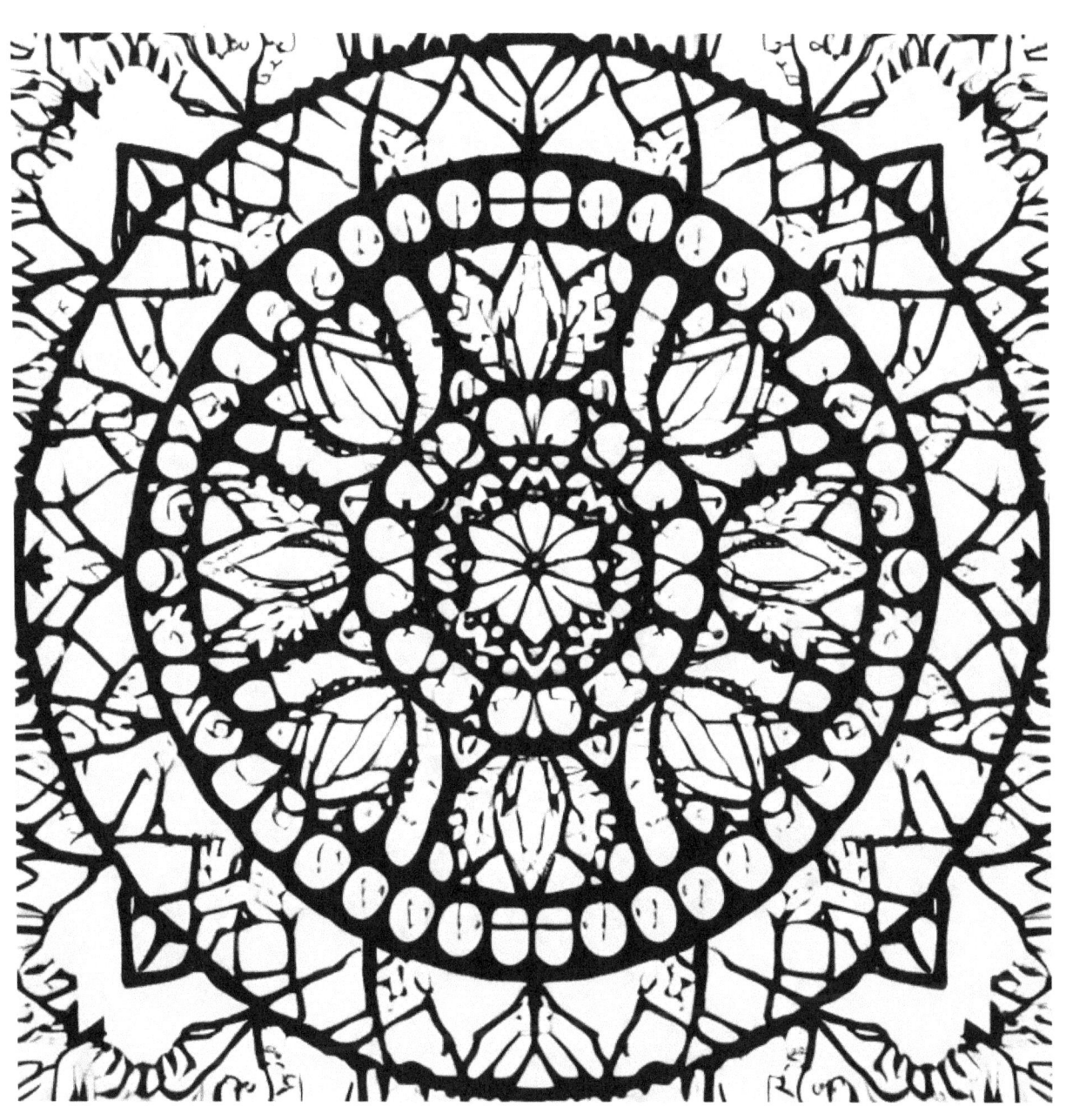

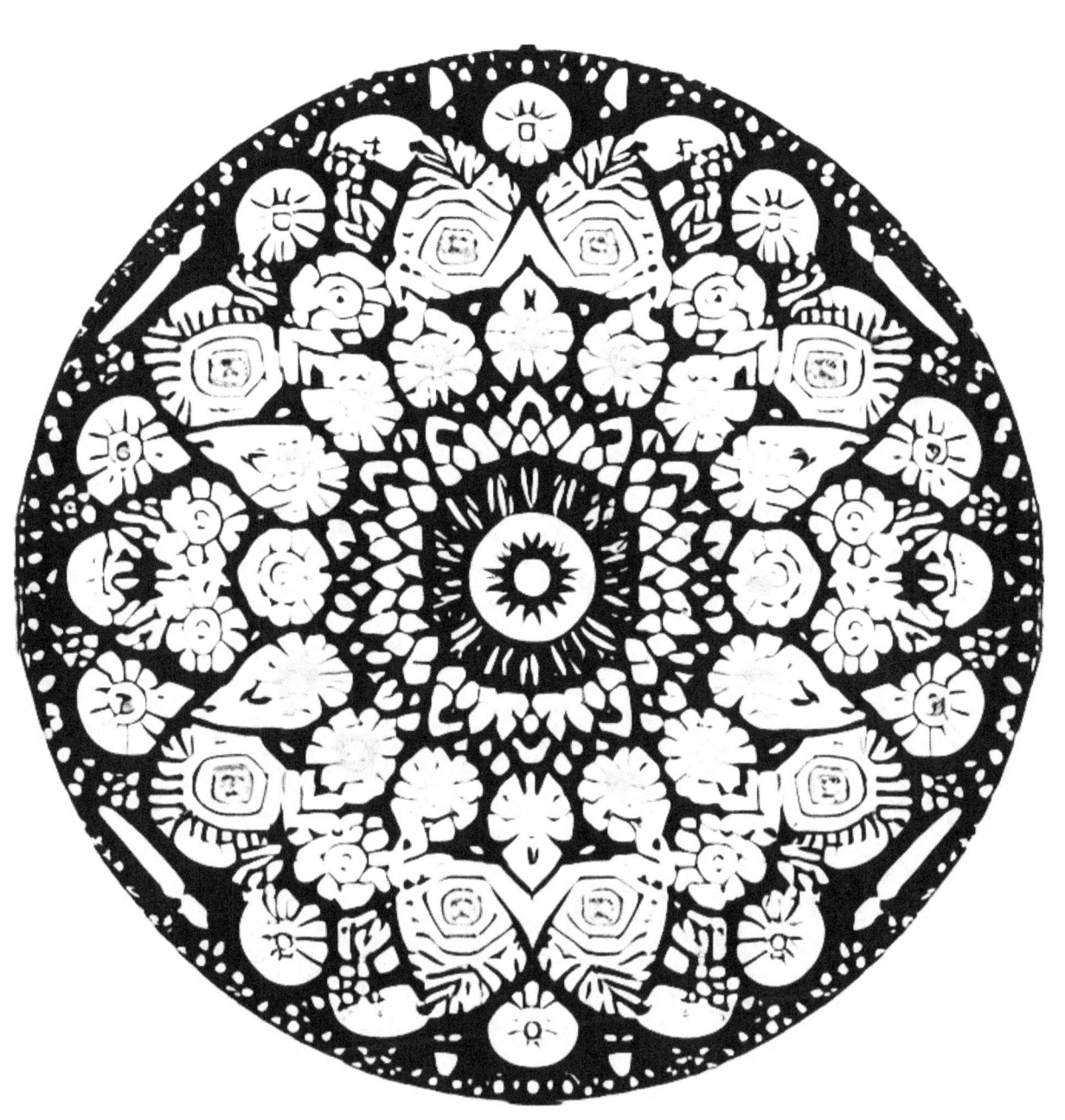

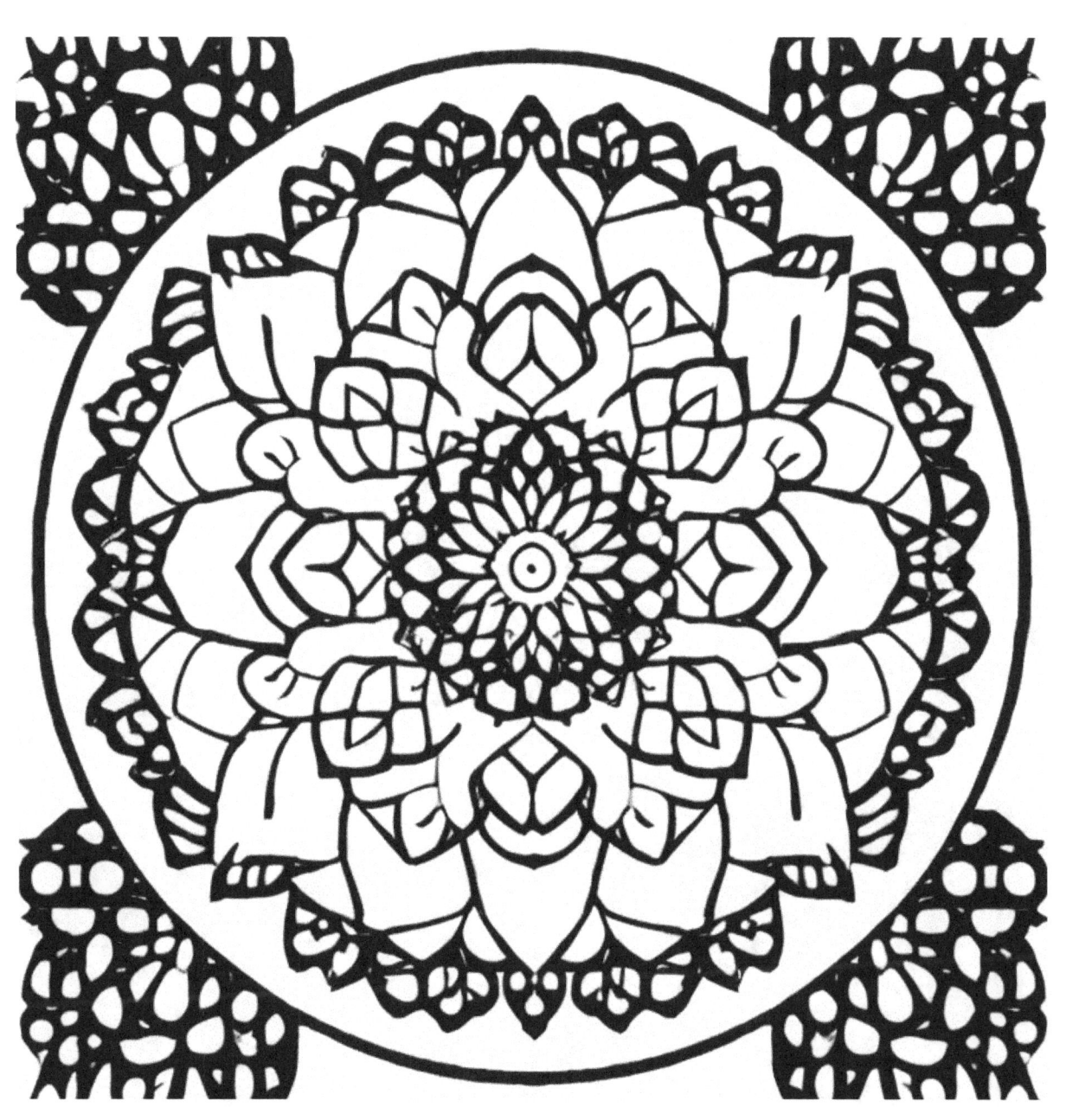

Thank you very much for purchasing this book. If you liked it, leave us a review please, when you can, regards Wilcher Eagle

www.ingramcontent.com/pod-product-compliance
Lightning Source LLC
Chambersburg PA
CBHW08083920526
45467CB00008B/2331